Ben Green

The irrepressible conflict between labor and capital

Ben Green

The irrepressible conflict between labor and capital

ISBN/EAN: 9783337235093

Printed in Europe, USA, Canada, Australia, Japan

Cover: Foto ©Suzi / pixelio.de

More available books at **www.hansebooks.com**

THE

IRREPRESSIBLE CONFLICT

BETWEEN

LABOR AND CAPITAL:

A BRIEF SUMMARY OF SOME OF THE CHIEF CAUSES AND
RESULTS OF THE LATE CIVIL WAR IN THE
UNITED STATES,

AS PRESENTED IN

THE TRANSLATOR'S PREFACE

TO

ADOLPHE GRANIER DE CASSAGNAC'S

HISTORY OF THE WORKING AND BURGHER CLASSES,

IN WHICH THE

ORIGIN, NATURE, AND OBJECTS OF THE MUCH CALUMNIATED

FRENCH COMMUNE

ARE HISTORICALLY EXPLAINED.

PHILADELPHIA:
CLAXTON, REMSEN & HAFFELFINGER,
819 & 821 MARKET STREET.
1872.

Translator's Dedication.

TO THE

WORKING AND BURGHER CLASSES OF AMERICA,

UNDER WHICH DESIGNATION I INCLUDE, NOT ONLY "LABORERS, MECHANICS,

HUSBANDMEN, AND MERCHANTS IN GENERAL," BUT ALSO LAWYERS,

PHYSICIANS, MINISTERS OF THE GOSPEL, AND ALL OTHERS

OF THE LEARNED PROFESSIONS, — ALL, WHO LIVE,

AND SEEK TO GROW RICH, BY THE FRUITS

OF THEIR OWN LABOR AND

INDUSTRY,

WHETHER OF THE HEAD,

OR OF THE HAND; AND NOT BY THE

"SUBTLE AND ARTFUL FISCAL CONTRIVANCES"

OF MODERN CLASS LEGISLATION, NOR BY PUBLIC OFFICE

AND PUBLIC PLUNDER, — THIS WORK IS RESPECTFULLY

Dedicated

By THE TRANSLATOR.

TRANSLATOR'S PREFACE.

F OR several years prior to the Civil War in America, the late STEPHEN COLWELL, of Philadelphia, withdrawing from active business, had shut himself up in his library, devoting himself principally to the study of Political Economy, on which subject his work on " The Ways and Means of Payment " is, perhaps, one of the ablest ever given to the public. Absorbed in this study from his own personal standpoint, that of a retired merchant and manufacturer, he gave little attention to matters of general politics occurring around him.

The news of the " Great Rebellion " reached him in the privacy of his library, and he again emerged into active life. Believing, like many other able and good men at the North, that the war was a " slaveholders' rebellion," and that everything should be sacrificed to the preservation of the Union, he took an active part in sustaining the Government. By degrees he became, under the excitements of the war, a thorough-going Abolitionist. He took great interest, and was one of the most active agents and liberal contributors, in sending teachers South to instruct the negroes.

When the war was over, he went to Paris, and again shut himself up in the libraries of that city. There he found De Cassagnac's " History of the Laboring and Burgher Classes." Struck with the great erudition of the work, and its peculiar views, he went to a book-dealer, and gave orders for the purchase of every copy that could be found for sale in Paris. It was out of print, and he could only secure three copies.

I met him in Philadelphia in 1868. In a brief interview, in which I gave him my views of the causes and results of the war, he paid me the compliment of saying that I had studied and understood the subject better than any one whom he had met; that he had brought this book from Paris to have it translated and published in the United States; that he was too old to do it himself, and had been looking for some one qualified for the task. He urged me to do it, and gave me the book.

Perhaps it is due to myself, and to my old preceptors of Georgetown College and the University of Virginia, to whose thorough training I am indebted for whatever merit there may be in the translation, that I should disarm the critics in advance, by an apology for any errors. Most of this work has been done hurriedly, under the pressure of much business and many cares, of my own and of others, at my home in Georgia, without access to dictionaries or books of reference, to compensate for twenty years' disuse of the Latin and Greek, and fifteen years' disuse of the French language; and I have sought always to give the author's exact meaning, sometimes perhaps sacrificing classic English to the exigencies of a close translation from the French.

This History was published in Paris in 1838, and is now for the first time offered to the American public. Heretofore it has been accessible to a very few only of the very few American readers of this class of French works. But through these few, some of the author's ideas, very soon after their publication in Paris, began to permeate into the American mind, and in course of time they became part of the political creed of a great party in the United States, resulting in the greatest and bloodiest civil war of recorded time.

De Cassagnac starts out with the declaration that his book is one of history, and not of politics. Evidently he was a student; poring over musty tomes; delighting in books, old and new; absorbed in the solution of the facts and philosophy of history. Certainly, so far as depends on ancient and modern law, history, and literature, he has in his seven years of preparatory study treated his subject exhaustively, and, as an historian, faithfully. But he probably little dreamed that in less than a quarter of a century, and on another continent, his ideas would take a new form of expression in the dogma that "free labor is cheaper than slave labor," and drench that continent in blood.

De Cassagnac dedicates his work to M. Guizot. Guizot was not a mere closet student. He was a statesman, intent on giving to the facts of history a gloss to suit the political purposes of the royal master, whose throne he sought to establish. He was the trusted minister of King Louis Philippe, whose every thought was directed to the perpetuation of his dynasty, and the repression of the "fierce democracie" of France. A translation of Guizot's Lectures on the History of Civilization was published in this country in 1838, about the time that De Cassagnac's book appeared in Paris. Those lectures were prepared for a special purpose: to strengthen the throne of Louis Philippe, by presenting to France *centralization and monarchy*, as represented by the Orleans dynasty, in their most attractive lights and colors. Guizot taxed his great abilities to the utmost to prove that "*whenever the reflection or the imagination of men has especially turned toward the contemplation or study of legitimate sovereignty, and of its essential qualities, it has inclined toward monarchy*," and that "*republicanism, under the most favorable circumstances, does not contain the principles of progress, duration, and extension.*"

Perhaps for the reason that the Americans are a more book-reading people than the French, it is probable that M. Guizot had more readers — and it is not going too far to say, more converts — in the United States than in France; and what was written with special reference to a political effect in France, exerted a potent influence in bringing about the civil war in America. M. Guizot has lived to see a great

2

party in the United States, under the name of that republicanism which he sought to disparage in France, preparing the way for that *centralization*, which, to use his language, "naturally and as if by instinct," inclines the minds of men to monarchy. Lest any of my readers should be startled at this assertion, and a prejudice be thereby aroused to hinder a dispassionate reception of what more I have to say, I ask, have they ever heard Mr. Sumner's lecture on "Are we a Nation?" and read M. Guizot's Lecture XI., on the "Centralization of Nations and Governments?"

Lest any of my readers may have fought under Grant or Sherman, and should throw down this book in disgust at the bare intimation that they carried fire and sword and famine into the South, in the interests of centralization and monarchy, let me here quote briefly from M. Guizot's eleventh lecture:

"Europe, however, was then (at the close of the fourteenth century) very far from understanding her own state, such as I have now endeavored to explain it to you. She did not know distinctly what she required, or what she was in search of, yet set about endeavoring to supply her wants as if she knew perfectly what they were. When the fourteenth century had expired, after the failure of every attempt at political organization, Europe entered, naturally and as if by instinct, into the path of centralization. It is the characteristic of the fifteenth century that it constantly tended to this result; that it endeavored to create general interests and general ideas; to raise the minds of men to more enlarged views; and to create, in short, what had not, till then, existed on a great scale — *nations* and governments.

"The actual accomplishment of this change belongs to the sixteenth and seventeenth centuries, though it was in the fifteenth that it was prepared. It is this preparation, this silent and hidden process of centralization, both in the social relations and in the opinions of men — a process accomplished, without premeditation or design, by the natural course of events — that we have now to make the subject of our inquiry.

"It is thus that man advances in the execution of a plan which he has not conceived, and of which he is not even aware. He is the free, intelligent artificer of a work, which is not his own. He does not perceive or comprehend it till it manifests itself by external appearances and real results ; and even then he comprehends it very imperfectly. It is through his means, however, and by the development of his intelligence and freedom, that it is accomplished. Conceive a great machine, the design of which is centred in a single mind, though its various parts are intrusted to different workmen, separated from and strangers to each other. No one of them understands the work as a whole, nor the general results, which he concurs in producing; but every one executes, with intelligence and freedom, by rational and voluntary acts, the particular task assigned to him. It is thus that by the hand of man the designs of Providence are wrought out in the government of the world. It is thus that the two great facts, which are apparent in the history of civilization, come to co-exist; on the one hand, those portions of it, which may be considered as fated, or which happen without the control of human knowledge or will ; on the other hand, the part played in it by the freedom and intelligence of man, and what he contributes to it by means of his own judgment and will."

When the true history of yet recent events shall have been written, many, who have been accustomed to believe that President Lincoln was the author and father of emancipation, will be surprised to learn that to the very last he was averse to it, and anxious to prevent the adoption of the Thirteenth Amendment to the Constitution, which was carried, not only without the concurrence of, but in direct opposition to, his judgment and will. When he visited Richmond, immediately after the evacuation in 1865, a message from my father, General Duff Green, asking an interview, reached him after

he had re-embarked and the command had already been
given to go ahead on the return to Washington. He immediately stopped the steamer, and waited for my father to come
aboard. When they met, Mr. Lincoln said, " My dear old
friend, how are you, and what can I do for you ? " My father
replied : " Mr. President, I went to see you at Springfield in
December, 1860, at the instance of Mr. Buchanan, and with
the concurrence of Mr. (Jefferson) Davis, to ask what you were
willing to do to avert the war. (a) I come now on my own account, to ask on what terms you are willing to grant us peace."
To this Mr. Lincoln said : " If the South want peace, all they
have to do is to lay down their arms and acknowledge the
authority of the Government of the United States. I cannot
recall my Emancipation Proclamations, but I am perfectly willing that the Supreme Court shall decide them to have been
unconstitutional, null, and void. If the South do not wish to
give up their slaves, let them call their Legislatures together,
and vote down the Thirteenth Amendment." The result of
this interview between my father and Mr. Lincoln, followed
up by another, in which Judge Campbell participated, was
that General Weitzel was authorized to call the Virginia
Legislature together, for the twofold purpose — first, of repeal-
ing the Act of Secession and recognizing the authority of
the General Government ; and, secondly, of voting down the
Thirteenth Amendment. On Mr. Lincoln's return to Washington, a pressure was brought to bear on him, that forced
him very reluctantly to cancel the authority given to General Weitzel to convene the Legislature. It is well known to
many that Mr. Lincoln was with great difficulty induced to
sign the Emancipation Proclamations. Perhaps no disputed
fact in history is susceptible of clearer proof. But few know
the historical fact that he was avowedly willing, and secretly
desired, that the Thirteenth Amendment should be defeated.

(a) See account of General Duff Green's visit to Mr. Lincoln, in the New York
Herald, of 8th January, 1861.

Much has been already, and ably, written on the causes that led to the late civil war. The ablest, who have written on the subject, are probably the Hon. Alexander H. Stephens, and Judge Nicholas, of Kentucky, whose views were condensed in a correspondence between them, published in the National Intelligencer, in the summer of 1868. Mr. Stephens said:

"Slavery so called, or that legal subordination of the black race to the white, which existed in all but one of the States when the Union was formed, and in fifteen of them when the war began, was unquestionably the occasion of the war, the main exciting proximate cause on both sides. But it was not the real cause, the *causa causans*, of it.

"The war grew out of different and directly opposite views as to the nature of the Government of the United States, and where, under our system, ultimate sovereign power, or paramount authority, properly resides."

"The truth is well established that the seceding States did not desire war. Very few of the public men in these States even expected war."

The gist of Judge Nicholas's rejoinder was that the question of the right of secession was the real cause of the war; that even a distinct recognition of rights in the Constitution could never be used for any available purpose; because, if at any time attempted to be exercised by a weaker portion of the country, the only result would be giving the Government the trouble of declaring war against and conquering it; that, as a remedy, the right of secession proved unavailable, and had to be abandoned; and that, therefore, expediency and policy required that the South should, by a total abnegation, deny that there was ever any legitimacy in their assertion of that right.

Mr. Stephens is, and Judge Nicholas was, a man of great force and ability. The former writes always in the spirit of a great constitutional lawyer and statesman. The argument of the latter on this occasion amounts simply to an assertion of the utter worthlessness of all constitutional guarantees; that might makes right; and that the weaker party, to avoid worse punishment, should always submit to whatever conditions the stronger thought proper to impose. On this occasion he sank far below himself; for on others he was unquestionably able. But with all deference to such authority, it must be said that neither have gone far enough back to discover the real causes of the war. Both agree that secession was adopted as a peaceful remedy — as a bloodless solution of pre-existing questions, involving the alternatives of civil war on the one hand, or submission to, what the weaker party believed to be, intolerable wrong on the other. How then can that be said to have been the real cause of the war, which was only resorted to as a peaceful remedy to prevent war?

We do not understand Mr. Stephens to mean that so many valuable lives were sacrificed, such heavy burdens imposed on both sections, merely to decide an abstract question of constitutional law; but only that the war would not have taken place when it did, if the North, under the lead of Massachusetts, had acquiesced *then* in the doctrine of State rights, including the right of secession, which Massachusetts asserted in the war of 1812, and on the acquisition of Louisiana.

The real causes of the war existed long before the right of secession was thought of in the South; long before it was asserted by Massachusetts; long before the Constitution or the Union was formed; long before New England began to grow rich by the importation and sale of negro slaves; and they still exist in full force, now that slavery has been abolished and the right of secession suppressed. They were —

1st. The irrepressible conflict between monarchy and democracy.

2d. The irrepressible desire of capital to cheapen labor.

From the beginning, the New England mind inclined to

monarchy, with established orders of nobility. Shortly before the adoption of the Constitution, John Adams, their greatest and favorite leader, with as much ability, with more zeal, and with less disguise than M. Guizot, published a defence of the New England ideas of government, from which the following are extracts:

" The people in all nations are naturally divided into two sorts, the gentlemen and the simple men, a word which is here chosen to signify the common people. By the common people we mean laborers, mechanics, husbandmen, and merchants in general, who pursue their occupations and industry without any knowledge in liberal arts and sciences, or in anything but their own trades and pursuits." (See John Adams's Defence of the Constitution, vol. iii., p. 458.)

"The distinctions.of poor and rich are as necessary in states of considerable extent (such as the United States) as labor and good government: the poor are destined to labor, and the rich, by the advantages of education, independence, and leisure, are qualified for superior stations." (Ibid., p. 360.)

" *A nobility must and will exist.* . . . Descent from certain parents and inheritance of certain houses, lands, and other visible objects (titles) will eternally have such an influence over the affections and imaginations of the people, as no arts and institutions will control. *Time will come, if it is not now,* that these circumstances will have more influence over great numbers of minds than any considerations of virtue and talents." (Vol. iii., p. 377.)

" The whole history of Rome shows that corruption began with the people sooner than the Senate." (Vol. iii., p. 327.)

" Powerful and crafty underminers have nowhere such rare sport as in a simple democracy, or single popular assembly. Nowhere, not in the completest despotism, does human nature show itself so completely depraved, so nearly approaching an equal mixture of brutality and devilishism, as in the

last stages of such a democracy, and in the beginning of despotism, which always succeeds it." (Ibid., vol. ii., p. 329.)

" It is the true policy of the common people to place the
whole executive power in the hands of one man." (Vol. iii.,
p. 460.)

" By kings and kingly power is meant the executive power
in a single person." (Vol. iii., p. 461.)

" There is not in the whole Roman history so happy a
period as this under their kings; . . . in short, Rome was
never so well governed or so happy." (Vol. iii., p. 305.)

" I only contend that the English Constitution is, in theory,
the most stupendous fabric of human invention. . . . In future
ages, if the present States become a great nation, their own
feelings and good sense will dictate to them what to do; they
may make *transitions* to a nearer resemblance of the British
Constitution." (Vol. i., pp. 70, 71.)

" It (the aristocracy) is a body of men which contains the
greatest collection of virtue and character in a free government; is the brightest ornament and glory of the nation, and
may always be made the greatest blessing of society, if it be
judiciously managed in the Constitution." (Vol. iii., p. 116.)

" Mankind have universally discovered that chance was
preferable to a corrupt choice, and have trusted Providence
rather than themselves. First magistrates and senators had
better be made hereditary at once, than that the people should
be universally debauched and bribed." (Vol. iii., p. 283.)

Such were the ideas to which the reflection and imagination of the leading men of New England inclined them at the
time of the adoption of that democratic form of government,
the denunciation of which as " a league with death and cove-
nant with hell," has been in vogue in New England down to
the time when that *transition* period, anticipated by their great
leader, commenced by amending the Constitution.

That these ideas have not lost ground in New England,
but have been spreading to the Middle and Western States,

appears by the following extract from the Monthly Gossip of Lippincott's Magazine for February, 1868:

"The *Revue de Quinzaine*, of October last, has a paper on Harvard University and Yale College, which shows a considerable knowledge of the subject. The writer says, that while the system and the division of studies are, in the main, the same as those of the English universities, yet important improvements have been introduced from time to time; and he truly remarks that, while Harvard has a certain aristocratic tone, in Yale the forms and the prevailing ideas are democratic. (*a*)

"The proposition recently made in Congress to tax the use of armorial bearings on carriages and household furniture is an eminently proper one, though it may perhaps cause some amusement at our expense in monarchical countries. If enacted into a law, the impost ought to yield a handsome return from New England, if one may judge from the fact that the *Heraldic Journal*, published by Wiggin & Lunt, Boston, has completed its third volume. A similar periodical in England, the *Herald and Genealogist*, edited by John Gough Nicholls, has also just completed its third volume, in the course of which there are five articles on 'Anglo-American genealogy and coat-armor.' The *New England Historical and Genealogical Register* has just issued its twenty-first volume, having started in 1847; and it is a curious fact that the New England Historic-Genealogical Society is the first one, particularly devoted to the pedigrees of families, ever formed. The interest which Americans take in this subject is also evinced by the increasing number of family histories which are issuing from the press. Heretofore these works were

(*a*) The truth of this statement, as to Harvard, is unquestionable; but if it be true that any democratic ideas prevail at Yale, the explanation of that phenomenon is to be found in the fact that, until recently, Yale has been mainly supported by students from the South and West, while Harvard was altogether sustained by New England.

mainly confined to New England and New York, which were settled before Pennsylvania and the Western States; but they are now appearing in other parts of the Union. Histories of the Sharpless, Darlington, Levering, Du Bois, Cope, Montgomery, Shippen, Wolfe, Coleman, and Hill families have been printed in this State, and those of the Buchanan and Sill families in Ohio. We hear that the pedigree of the Wentworth family is about to be published in Chicago; and that Mr. D. Williams Patterson, of Pittston, Pennsylvania, has in preparation the genealogy of the Grant family, which will include the pedigree of General Ulysses S. Grant. It appears that his ancestor was Matthew Grant, whose name first occurs on the town records of Dorchester, Massachusetts, April 3, 1633. Noah, the grandfather of the General, born in Connecticut, June 20, 1748, and the sixth generation in descent from the Dorchester emigrant, came from Coventry, Connecticut, to Pennsylvania, after the Revolutionary War, and settled here. The Rev. Mr. Headley's statement, that the ancestor of Grant settled in Pennsylvania on his arrival in this country, is therefore erroneous. Although very frequently indeed these pedigrees are fit subjects of ridicule, some link in a chain being assumed without proof, or some sign of vanity being exhibited by the degenerate offspring of worthy sires; yet at the bottom of all this there is, on the whole, a healthy family-pride, which benefits society, and to which no one, who comes of virtuous and honorable parentage, is insensible."

Speaking of an *elective* chief-magistrate, Mr. Adams said, " This hazardous experiment the Americans have tried, and if elections are soberly made, it may answer very well; but if parties, factions, drunkenness, bribes, *armies*, and delirium come in, as they have always done, sooner or later, to embroil and decide everything, the people must again have recourse to conventions, and find a remedy for this ' hazardous experiment.' Neither philosophy nor policy has yet discovered any other cure than by prolonging the duration of the first magistrate and senators. The evil may be lessened and postponed by elections for longer periods of years, until they become for life ; and if this is not found an adequate remedy, there will remain no other but to make them hereditary." (Vol. iii., p. 296.)

Observe that Mr. Adams also said, " *The time will come, if it is not now;* " and among the signs of the time he enumerated " bribes, armies, and delirium." In this connection, the organization of the " Grand Army of the Republic," and the establishment of the *Imperialist* newspaper in New York, just after the war, to test whether the time had come for the realization of these views, by making General Grant emperor, are signs of the time not to be overlooked. The " Grand Army of the Republic," with all its commanderies and commanders, has so far only served to strengthen the Democratic vote, by a reaction from the delirium of the war ; and the *Imperialist* newspaper expired with the death of General Rawlings, Grant's Secretary of War. (*a*) This, however, does not prove that the monarchical and aristocratic spirit of New England is dead, but only that the time has not yet come.

But there were in New England then, as now, some

(*a*) Of all the converts to the logic of Adams and Guizot, General Rawlings was perhaps the most sincere, the purest, the least influenced by selfish considerations. He had come to believe that Rome was never so well governed or so happy as under her kings, and that the good government and happiness of this vast country required that it should be centralized into a *nation* and governed by an emperor. There is reason to believe that his death was hastened by chagrin at finding out that General Grant, whom he had selected as the instrument for that *transition*, was not the right man. Bribes and armies are potent for the subversion of democratic government and the establishment of empires ; but the former must be given, not received, by the aspirant for imperial sway. Plutarch relates of Sylla that, while prætor, he happened to be provoked at (Sextus Julius) Cæsar, and said to him, angrily, " I will use *my* authority against you." Cæsar answered, laughing, " You do well to call it *yours*, for you *bought* it." Whether true or false, it soon came to be believed of General Grant that he was more ready to *sell* than to *buy* his authority.

earnest and able advocates of free government, as, for instance, Samuel Adams. The sentiment against monarchy was so strong in other portions of the Union, and especially in the slaveholding States of the South, that after the adoption of the Constitution, the monarchical party deemed it prudent to assume the name of Federalists, as being less unpopular than one more indicative of their peculiar ideas and theories of government. In the Boston Monthly Anthology, for March, 1807, the curious reader will find some verses (a) denunciatory of the Republican party, in which this policy of assuming a name for political purposes is thus referred to:

> "And if we cannot alter things,
>   By G—, we 'll change their *names*, sir!
>   .   .   .   .
> True, Tom and Joel now no more
>   Can overturn a nation:
> And work by butchery and blood,
>   A great regeneration, —
> Yet, still we can turn inside out
>   Old nature's constitution,
> And bring a Babel back of *names*, —
> Huzza! for REVOLUTION."

The advocates of the Constitution as adopted were, and called themselves, Republicans; but their opponents in New England called them Democrats in derision. In course of time they accepted this name, as indicative of their theory that legitimate sovereignty resides in the whole body of the people, and not in a king and nobility; and, as soon as they dropped the name of Republicans for that of Democrats, their opponents, the monarchists, took it up, and assumed it as their own party appellation.

During the session of Congress of 1807–8, Mr. John Q.

(a) The authorship of these verses was attributed, and no doubt correctly, to John Quincy Adams. By Tom and Joel, Tom Paine and Joel Barlow, anti-monarchists, were referred to.

Adams surprised his former political opponents as well as his own party friends, by what Governor Giles, of Virginia, in an address to the public, dated February 28, 1828, calls "a complete political somerset from the Federal (or monarchical) to the Republican (or democratic) party." In explanation of his course, Mr. Adams told Governor Giles and Mr. Jefferson that the object of the Federal (or monarchical) party in New England "had been for several years the dissolution of the Union and the establishment of a separate confederacy; that he knew this from unequivocal evidence, although not provable in a court of justice; and that, in case of a civil war, the aid of Great Britain to effect that purpose would be as surely resorted to as it would be indispensably necessary to the design." (a)

The following is an extract from a letter from Mr. Jefferson to Governor Giles, dated Monticello, December 26, 1825:

"You ask my opinion of the propriety of giving publicity to what is stated in your letter, as having passed between John Q. Adams and yourself. Of this no one can judge but yourself. It is one of those questions which belong to the forum of feeling. This alone can decide on the degree of confidence implied in the disclosure: whether, under no circumstances, it was to be communicable to others. It does not seem to be of that character, or at all to meet that aspect. They are historical facts, which belong to the present as well as future time. I doubt whether a single fact, known to the world, will carry as clear a conviction to it, of the correctness of our knowledge of the treasonable views of the Federal party of that day, as that disclosed by this most nefarious and daring attempt to dissever the Union, of which the Hartford Convention was a subsequent chapter; and both of these having failed, *consolidation* becomes the first book of their history. But this opens with a vast accession of strength,

(a) See Mr. Adams's own statement in National Intelligencer, October 21, 1828.

from their younger recruits, who, having nothing in them of the feelings or principles of '76, now look to a single and splendid government of an aristocracy, founded on banking institutions and moneyed incorporations, under the guise and cloak of their favored branches of manufactures, commerce, and navigation, riding and ruling over the plundered ploughman and beggared yeomanry. This will be to them a next best blessing to the monarchy of their first aim, and perhaps the surest stepping-stone to it."

When it was made known that Mr. John Quincy Adams, in explaining to Governor Giles and Mr. Jefferson his reasons for joining the Republican or Democratic party, had charged these treasonable views upon the Federal party of New England, some of his late political associates, who claimed to be patriots, while conscientiously believing the monarchical form of government the best, retorted on him, by charging that he was still a monarchist at heart, and that his conversion to democracy was only pretended. They asserted that " in 1807, at the table of an illustrious citizen now no more, he (Mr. Adams) *lamented* the fearful progress of the Democratic party and of its principles, and declared that ' *he had long meditated the subject, and had become convinced that the only method, by which the Democratic party could be destroyed, was by joining with it, and urging it on with the utmost energy to the completion of its views: whereby the result would prove so ridiculous, and so ruinous to the country, that the people would be led to despise the principles and to condemn the effects of Democratic policy; and* THEN,' *said he,* ' WE MAY HAVE A FORM OF GOVERNMENT BETTER SUITED TO THE GENIUS AND DISPOSITION OF OUR COUNTRY THAN OUR PRESENT CONSTITUTION." (a)

This charge made against Mr. John Quincy Adams by his then late associates was denied; and the attempt was made to prove it by the affidavits of Messrs. Townsend and Derby, of the monarchical party, both men of high standing in Mas-

(a) See Boston Statesman, November, 1824.

sachusetts.   The case made by these affidavits against Mr.
Adams was strong, but not conclusive, although they after-
ward acquired much additional force from Mr. Adams's subsequent reaffiliation with the party whom his father, John Adams,
in one of his letters to Cunningham, styles the *"Absolute Oli-
garchy,"* and by the bitterness of his hatred of Democracy,
and of its stronghold, the Southern slaveholding States.

But whether the charge was true or false — whether this
idea originated with John Quincy Adams, or with the monarchical party, who brought the charge of having originated
it against him, certain it is that they have since then pushed
it vigorously and successfully.   For what can be more or
better calculated to "lead the people to despise the principles
and to condemn the effects of Democratic policy," than to see a
parcel of ignorant negroes, recently slaves, with no knowledge
of history or jurisprudence, controlling the destinies of States
like Virginia and South Carolina, in the place of such men
as George Washington, Thomas Jefferson, Madison, Sumter,
Marion, and Calhoun?

New England was not only monarchical.   She was also a
negro-slave trader; and it was not until it was discovered
that the effect of negro slavery was to strengthen the democratic principle of equality among the whites, that negro
slavery became odious to New England.   In course of time,
it was seen that the ownership of negro slaves carried with it
the necessity of making color and good conduct (not wealth
and poverty) the only basis for distinction.   In the presence
of their black slaves and of the poor white men, whom they
employed as overseers, and whose authority it was necessary
to maintain, the slave-owners found themselves compelled to
treat the poor white man as an equal, because he was white,
and the negro slave as an inferior, because he was black.   In
no other way could they teach the negroes lessons of obedience to their poor white overseers, or keep up the personal
pride, self-respect, and character of the overseers, which was

indispensable, that they might more easily control the slaves. When, at a later period, the Southern slaveholders learned • that Old England was seeking to abolish slavery in the United States, as a means of securing for her own East-India possessions a monopoly of the production of cotton and sugar, and that the monarchists and aristocrats of New England had united with Old England against them, they found it more than ever necessary to strengthen themselves by inculcating upon their children and neighbors that color and good conduct were the only proper foundation for *castes*.

It was this *necessity* of the slave-owners — the necessity of employing poor white men as overseers, and of treating them with respect in the presence of the negro slaves, so as to secure respect and obedience to them from the slaves—which, perhaps more than all else, led to the marked contrast between the social relations and distinctions in the non-slaveholding and in the slaveholding States. In the former, if a laboring man had occasion to call at the house of a rich man, he was kept standing at the front door, or at best in the passage-way, until his business was accomplished. In the latter, he was invited to be seated in the parlor; was offered a glass of wine, or whisky and water; was asked to dinner, if that hour was nigh; his family and business affairs, the weather, the crops and politics were discussed, as between equals and friends. M. Guizot, in his History of Civilization, comments on, and attaches great importance to, an analogous effect of the Crusades on the social relations of Europe. He says:

"During the Crusades, small proprietors found it necessary to place themselves in the train of some rich and powerful chief, from whom they received assistance and support. They lived with him, shared his fortune, and passed through the same adventures that he did. When the Crusaders returned home, *this social spirit, this habit of living in intercourse with superiors*, continued to subsist, and had its influence on the manners of the age. . . .

"Such, in my opinion, are the real effects of the Crusades: on the one hand, the extension of ideas and the emancipation of thought; on the other, a general enlargement of the social sphere, and an opening of a wider field for every sort of activity; they produced, at the same time, more individual freedom and more political unity."

Such was the effect of negro slavery in the South on the social relations of the rich and poor whites.

I remember, when a boy, hearing the striking contrast between the social relations of the rich and poor whites at the South and at the North, commented upon by my father. It was before the days of railroads, when travelling was by stage coach, and before the Abolition agitation had begun to attract attention. He had always lived in the South, and was accustomed to the social equality among the whites there prevailing. In a tour through the Northern States, he rode generally with the stage-driver, to see the country. At the first meal-stand in Pennsylvania, he was struck with the fact, that the *white* stage-driver was not permitted to take his seat at the same table with the passengers; and, as he progressed northward, he found the rule universal that, in the non-slaveholding States, the driver was required to eat at a separate and inferior table. He was long enough in the Northern and Eastern States to become somewhat familiarized with this distinction there made between the rich passengers and the poor drivers; and as he passed through Maryland on his return, he did not notice whether the driver was permitted to eat at the passengers' table or not. From Washington City he started on a similar tour through the Southern States. The first day out in Virginia, he reached the meal-stand with a traveller's appetite, and, seeing dinner ready, he was about to take his seat; but was stopped and told by the waiter that the passengers must wait until the driver — a white man — who was washing his hands, was ready to take his seat with them. This little circumstance caused him to be more observant of

3

the absence of the New-England social distinction between the poor and the rich, and of this social equality among the whites, which he found everywhere a prominent characteristic of the slaveholding States.

From having heard my father speak of this, now nearly thirty years ago, and often since, my own attention was called to it, and in a very extensive observation in all the slaveholding States, I have found it universal, and more strongly developed as the Abolition agitation progressed. Shortly before the war, I was visiting one of the largest slaveholders, (a) a truly representative man of his class, who had a poor white neighbor employed digging a well. When the first bell rang for the ladies to dress for dinner, this well-digger came out of his hole in the ground, washed and dressed himself, took his seat at the table with the family and guests, and seemed as much at his ease as if he had been governor of the State.

This privilege of color could be forfeited by bad conduct, and by bad conduct only; and when so lost, the negro slaves despised the losers, and spoke of them contemptuously as "mean white trash;" sometimes as "poor white trash;" not because they were *poor*, but because, being white, they had forfeited by misconduct the respect due to them by virtue of their white skins.

This tendency of negro slavery, as it existed in the South, to break down "the distinctions of rich and poor" whites, which the monarchical - aristocratic party of New England held to be "as necessary in states of considerable extent (such as the United States) as labor and good government," gave a great impulse to the agitation against negro slavery, which had been originally set on foot by paid agents of Old England, with a view of securing a monopoly of the pro-

(a) The planter here alluded to was the late Colonel Andrew P. Calhoun, eldest son of John C. Calhoun; and the well-digger's name was, I think, Boggs, of Pickens District, South Carolina.

duction of cotton and sugar for the British East-India possessions.

But there was another remarkable tendency of negro slavery, which made it still more odious to those who desired a transition to a nearer resemblance of the "British Constitution," and therefore "lamented the fearful progress of the Democratic party and of its principles." This was its political effect on the character of the poor whites, or "common people," of the South. Their social elevation, the more respectful treatment secured to them by the *necessity* of the slaveowners, as above explained, increased their self-respect, and caused them to value more highly their political franchises, which, at the same time, made them the superiors of the negroes, and the political, as well as social, equals of their rich white neighbors. For this reason bribery at elections was a thing almost unknown at the South. Even the most abject of those, whom the very negro slaves despised as "poor white trash," recoiled from that lower depth of degradation — selling his vote. This was strikingly illustrated by the testimony elicited by the Covode Investigating Committee, 1st Session, 36th Congress, vol. v., p. 490. It there appears that bribery at elections had grown to be a customary thing with all parties in the free States. The witness, a Northern man, being asked, "Have all your contributions been in Northern States?" replied, "Yes, sir; I do not remember spending a dollar politically in Southern States. I have tendered contributions there, but they allowed they did not use money as we use it·in the Northern States."

In course of time, another remarkable result of negro slavery was developed and came to be understood by the master minds of W. H. Seward, Salmon P. Chase, and a few others, although the great majority of the free and intelligent artificers of the work, which they designed, did not perceive or comprehend it, while executing the particular tasks assigned to them, and even now comprehend it very incom-

pletely. Mr. Seward misled the productive classes of the
free States by the specious dogma of "an irrepressible conflict
between free labor and slave labor," when in fact there was
no such conflict; the interests of all labor, whether free or
slave, being identical, viz., to keep up wages and keep down
the cost of living. The real conflict was — not between free
and slave labor — but it was between the capital that hired
free labor, and the capital that owned slave labor. The
interests of the former required a system of legislation that
would put down wages and put up the cost of living. The
interests of the latter required a diametrically opposite system.
Wages went into, and the cost of living came out of, the
pockets of the capital that owned slave labor. Wages came
out of, and the cost of living went into, the pockets of the
capital, that hired free labor. Mr. Seward and Mr. Chase
were not long in discovering that herein consisted the philosophy of Mr. Jefferson's celebrated aphorism, "The Democracy of the North are the natural allies of the Republicans of the South." They were not slow to see that, while
the interests and inclination of the capital that hired free labor
called for a system of taxation imposing heavy burdens on
the laboring classes, the interests and inclination of the
capital that owned slave labor required a system of light
taxes, high wages, fair prices for the products of labor, and
cheap living. While many of their less discerning "workmen" were surprised to see the Southern slaveholders voting
and exerting their influence to shape the legislation of the
country to this end, and were astonished that those whom
they were taught to consider as the "slave aristocracy,"
should thus act *against* the interests of those whom they
were taught to consider the *true* aristocracy, and *for* the interests of the "common people," (the laboring and productive classes of the North,) Mr. Seward's astute mind solved
the mystery. He saw that one peculiar result of negro
slavery was to identify the interests of the Southern slave-

holders and of the northern working-men ; that it gave to Northern labor in its conflict with Northern capital — to the "laborers, mechanics, husbandmen, and merchants in general" of the North in their conflict with the aristocracy — a potent ally in the slaveholders of the South ; that it joined them together, as the priest joins man and wife, and that to abolish slavery would be to *divorce* Southern capital from Northern labor.

[Since the foregoing was written, Mr. Attorney-General Akerman has been to Washington City, and was initiated into the counsels of those, in whose minds the designs of the Government machine are centred. Returning to Georgia, he made a speech in Representatives' Hall, Atlanta, 1st September, 1870, by which it clearly appears that, among other things learned by him in the Cabinet councils, was this fact: that one of the main objects and results of the war was to *divorce* Southern capital from Northern labor. His speech, whether prepared by him or for him, evinces much adroitness in view of the objects to be accomplished by it. They were, first, to call the attention of Southern capital to the fact, that it is no longer interested in opposing high taxes, low wages and prodigal Government expenditures ; that it has no longer any interests in common with the laboring classes, the "common people," of the North ; secondly, to prepare the way for an election bill, by which the ignorant negroes of Georgia, voting early and often, on several different days and in several different counties, could be used to neutralize the votes of intelligent white Democratic workmen in Ohio or Pennsylvania. He said:

" My friends, I am touching now a serious topic. . . . In the United States, looking at the white population alone, the cry of a conflict between capital and labor has generally been the cry of the demagogue, for the reason that capital has seldom been organized against labor, and labor has seldom, except in the small way of trades' unions, been organized against capital. . . .

"*How is the problem affected by the elevation of colored men to freedom ? Labor and capital were in the same hands here in the South. They have now become* DIVORCED *by emancipation.*"]

In a speech, at Boston, shortly before the inauguration of President Lincoln, Mr. Seward avowed that, in his theories of government, he was a disciple of John Adams. The quotations we have given from Mr. Adams's book show what those theories were. Mr. Seward, then, believed that "a nobility must and will exist;" that "the aristocracy is the brightest ornament and glory of the nation;" that "first-magistrates and senators had better be made hereditary at once, than that the people should be universally debauched and bribed;" that "the distinctions of poor and rich are as necessary in states of considerable extent (such as the United States) as labor and good government;" and that these States, having become a great nation, should "make transitions to a nearer resemblance of the British Constitution." (*a*) But a thorough, statesman-like, philosophic investigation of the social and political effects of negro slavery in the South also disclosed to him the fact, that its tendencies were all anti-monarchical and anti-aristocratic ; that the slaveholder was surrounded by necessities, which, in his social treatment of his poor white neighbor, forced him to become what John Adams would call a "vulgar democrat," (*b*) and in his political action forced him to vote with the "common people," and against the monarchical aristocracy of the North, for light taxes, high wages, and cheap living ; and, seeing this, he declared that "these States must become all free;" that negro slavery must be abolished, and capital *divorced* from labor.

M. Guizot says :

"The struggle of classes constitutes the very fact of

(*a*) Query : Russian ?
(*b*) See John Adams's Letters to Cunningham.

modern history, of which it is full. Modern Europe, indeed, is born of this struggle between the different classes
of society." (*a*)

The same is true of the United States. We see this struggle of classes in Mr. Adams's book; we see it in the dogma
of the political party that elected Mr. Lincoln and made war
on the South to abolish slavery, that "free labor might be
made cheaper than slave labor;" we see it in Chief-Justice
Chase's son-in-law's declaration at the Memphis Commercial
Convention that labor must be cheapened; (*b*) we see it in
the substitution of negro for white printers in the Government printing-office at Washington City; we see it in the
attempt to *cheapen* the labor of shoemakers in Massachusetts
and negroes in the South by the substitution and competition
of the "heathen Chinese;" we see it in the trades' unions
of the North, and in the National Labor Union of the United
States.

It has long been held by a certain class of statesmen that
the United States could never take that rank among nations,
to which their vast territory and great resources entitle them,
without manufactures; and that they cannot compete with
Europe in manufactures without reducing the wages of labor
in the United States to the standard of wages in Europe.
Among the living advocates of cheap labor, we again find
Mr. Seward and Chief-Justice Chase the ablest. The only
difference between them, in this respect, is that Mr. Seward,
residing in the East, was a high-tariff man, seeking to cheapen
labor, by taxing labor for the benefit of the capital that employed labor, as well as by abolishing slavery; while Mr.
Chase, though born and educated in New England, moved in
early life to the West, where the protection theories were

(*a*) See Guizot's History of Civilization, D. Appleton & Co., New York,
1837, p. 184.
(*b*) See Senator Sprague's speech at the Memphis Convention.

unpopular, and therefore relied mainly on abolition to cheapen labor.

In searching for the origin of the dogma that "free labor may be made cheaper than slave labor," I find it in M. de Cassagnac's book. He proves, demonstratively, that all voluntary emancipations on a large scale have been made for the benefit of the master, to get rid of the care and expense of supporting the slaves; and that the invariable result of all emancipations has been to produce four classes, viz., hirelings, beggars, prostitutes, and thieves. The corollary is that pauperism increases competition in the struggle for the means of existence, and increased competition tends to a further reduction of wages, below the cost of feeding and clothing a slave, and taking care of him in infancy, sickness, and old age.

About the same time, viz., in 1837, Mr. Calhoun, in his speech on the reception of Abolition petitions, threw out, with less elaboration, similar ideas: that the tendency of negro slavery in the South was to strengthen the principle of republican equality among the whites, and that no laboring class in any part of the world were so well treated and cared for, or received so large a share of the products of their labor, as the negro slaves of the South. He said:

"I appeal to facts. Never before has the black race of Central Africa, from the dawn of history to the present day, attained a position so civilized and so improved, not only physically, but morally and intellectually. It came among us in a low, degraded, and savage condition; and, in the course of a few generations, it has grown up under the fostering care of our institutions, as reviled as they have been, to its present comparative civilized condition. This, with the rapid increase of numbers, is conclusive proof of the general happiness of the race, in spite of all the exaggerated tales to the contrary.

"In the mean time, the white or European race has not

degenerated. It has kept pace with its brethren in other sections of the Union, where slavery does not exist. It is odious to make comparisons; but I appeal to all sides whether the South is not equal in virtue, intelligence, patriotism, courage, disinterestedness, and all the high qualities, which adorn our nature. I ask whether we have not contributed our full share of talents and political wisdom in forming and sustaining this political fabric? and *whether we have not constantly inclined most strongly to the side of liberty, and been the first to see, and first to resist the encroachments of power.* In one thing only are we inferior — the arts of gain : we acknowledge that we are less wealthy than the Northern section of this Union ; but I trace this mainly to the fiscal action of this Government, which has extracted much from and spent little among us. Had it been the reverse — if the exaction had been from the other section, and the expenditure with us — this point of superiority would not be against us now, as it was not at the formation of this Government.

"But I take higher ground. I hold that, in the present state of civilization, where two races of different origin, and distinguished by color and other physical differences, as well as intellectual, are brought together, the relation now existing in the slave-holding States between the two is, instead of an evil, a good — a positive good. I feel myself called upon to speak freely upon the subject, where the honor and interests of those I represent are involved. I hold, then, that there never has yet existed a wealthy and civilized society in which one portion of the community did not, in point of fact, live on the labor of the other. Broad and general as is this assertion, it is fully borne out by history. This is not the proper occasion; but if it were, it would not be difficult to trace the various devices, by which the wealth of all civilized communities has been so unequally divided, and to show by what means so small a share has been allotted to those, by whose labor it was produced, and so large a share given to the non-producing class. The devices are almost innumerable, from the brute force and gross superstition of ancient times to the subtle and artful fiscal contrivances of modern. I might well challenge a comparison between them and the more direct, simple, and patriarchal mode, by which the labor of the African race is among us commanded by the European. I may say, with truth, that in few countries so much is left to the share of the laborer, and so little exacted from him, or where there is more kind attention to him in sickness or infirmities of age. Compare his condition with the tenants of the poor-houses in the most civilized portions of Europe. Look at the sick, and the old and infirm slave, on the one hand, in the midst of his family and friends, under the kind superintend-ing care of his master and mistress, and compare it with the forlorn and wretched condition of the pauper in the poor-house. But I will not dwell on this aspect of the question. I turn to the political; and here I fearlessly assert, that the existing relation between the two races in the South, against which those blind fanatics are waging war, forms the most solid and durable foundation on which to rear free and stable political institutions. It is useless to disguise the fact. There is and always has been, in an advanced stage of wealth and civilization, a conflict between labor and capital. The condi-tion of society in the South exempts us from the disorders and dangers resulting from this conflict; and this explains why it is that the political condition of the slaveholding States has been so much more stable and quiet than the North. The advantages of the former in this respect will become more and more manifest, if left undisturbed by inter-ference from without, as the country advances in wealth and numbers. We have, in fact, but just entered that condition of society where the strength and durability of our political in-stitutions are to be tested; and I venture nothing in predict-ing that the experience of the next generation will fully test how vastly more favorable our condition of society is to that of other sections for free and stable institutions, provided we are not disturbed by the interference of others, or shall have sufficient intelligence and spirit to resist promptly and successfully such interferences. It rests with ourselves to meet and repel them.

" Be assured that emancipation itself would not satisfy these fanatics; that gained, the next step would be to raise the negroes to a social and political equality with the whites; and that being effected, we would soon find the present condition of the two races reversed. They and their Northern allies would be the masters, and we the slaves; the condition of the white race in the British West Indies, as bad as it is, would be happiness to ours. There the mother country is interested in sustaining the supremacy of the European race. It is true that the authority of the former master is destroyed, but the African will there be a slave, not to individuals, but to the community; forced to labor, not by the authority of the overseer, but by the bayonet of the soldiery and the rod of the civil magistrate."

Mr. Calhoun was an ardent, a passionate devotee of the Union under the Constitution; and it is questionable whether Governor Joseph E. Brown, of Georgia, could have succeeded in hurrying the Southern States into secession in 1861, if Mr. Calhoun had then been living. Entering public life in 1811, he was one of the ablest and most zealous supporters of the war of 1812 with Great Britain, in defence of the rights and interests of the seamen of New England; and his earnest nature was soon shocked by discovering that the object of the so-called Federal party in New England "had been, for several years, the dissolution of the Union and the establishment of a separate confederacy," by the co-operation of Great Britain.(a) The study of his life, therefore, was to find in the Constitution some balance-wheel, or regulator, which would

(a) See statement of John Quincy Adams in the National Intelligencer, October 21, 1828.

guard against the danger of secession on the one hand, or centralization and despotism on the other.   Hence his modification of Mr. Jefferson's doctrine of *nullification*, as an antidote to the New England doctrine of the right of secession,(*a*)

(*a*) The doctrine of *nullification*, as laid down in the Virginia and Kentucky Resolutions, and as maintained by Jefferson, Madison, and others, made *each* State, *for itself and separately*, the judge of any alleged infraction of the Constitution, and of the " *mode and measure of redress.*"

Mr. Calhoun's modification of that doctrine proposed to make " *all the States in convention assembled* " the judge ; and meanwhile, until such a convention of *all* the States could be called together for the decision of the question, to give to each State the right to nullify, or *suspend* the execution of an obnoxious and unconstitutional law *temporarily* within her borders.   By this State right of temporary suspension, analogous to the Presidential veto, Calhoun sought to protect the weaker States from hasty and unjust legislation ; while he relied on the calm deliberations of a convention of *all* the States to effectually suppress the spirit of secession.

Mr. Thomas Ritchie, of the Richmond Enquirer, Mr. Francis P. Blair, of the Washington Globe, the National Intelligencer, and others, admitting the right of secession, opposed Mr. Calhoun's modification of the doctrine of the Kentucky and Virginia Resolutions, on the ground that its effect would be to place a State *in* the Union and *out of* the Union at the same time.   See Calhoun's address to the people of South Carolina. (Jenkins's Life of Calhoun, pp. 172–173.) He said :

" How the States are to exercise this high power of interposition, which constitutes so essential a portion of their reserved rights that it *cannot be delegated without an entire surrender of their sovereignty*, and converting our system from a *federal* into a *consolidated* government, is a question that the States only are competent to determine.   The arguments, which prove that they possess the power, equally prove that they are, in the language of Jefferson, ' *the rightful judges of the mode and measure of redress.*'   But the spirit of forbearance, as well as the nature of the right itself, forbids a recourse to it, except in cases of dangerous infractions of the Constitution ; and then only in the last resort, when all reasonable hope of relief from the ordinary action of the Government has failed ; when, if the right to interpose did not exist, the alternative would be submission and oppression on one side, or resistance by force on the other.   That our system should afford, in such extreme cases, an intermediate point between these dire alternatives, by which the Government may be brought to a pause, and thereby an interval obtained to compromise differences, or, if impracticable, be compelled to submit the question to a constitutional adjustment, through an appeal to the States themselves, is an evidence of its high wisdom ; an element, not, as is supposed by some, of weakness, but of strength : not of anarchy or revolution, but and to the New England spirit of centralization and monarchy. His last words in the Senate of the United States, when the hand of death was upon him; — when the ambition of this world was over; — were a plea for the Union under the Constitution.   His speech of 1837, from which we have just quoted, was an earnest and able appeal to the justice, good sense, and self-interests of the laboring and productive classes of the North, for the Union under the Constitution, against the Abolitionists, then few in number and generally regarded

of peace and safety. *Its general recognition would, in a great measure, if not altogether, supersede the necessity of its exercise, by impressing on the movements of the Government that moderation and justice so essential to harmony and peace, in a country of such vast extent and diversity of interests as ours;* and would, if controversy should come, turn the resentment of the aggrieved from the system to those who had abused its powers, (a point all-important,) and cause them to seek redress, *not in revolution or overthrow, but in reformation.* It is, in fact, properly understood, *a substitute, where the alternative would be force, tending to prevent, and, if that fails, to correct peaceably the aberrations, to which all systems are liable, and which, if permitted to accumulate, without correction, must finally end in a general catastrophe.*"

See also Calhoun's letter to Governor Hamilton, of 28th August, 1832, in which he said :

" If the views presented be correct, it follows that on the interposition of a State in favor of the reserved rights, it would be the duty of the General Government to abandon the contested power, or to apply to the States themselves, the source of all political authority, for the power, in one of the two modes prescribed by the Constitution.   If the case be a simple one, embracing a single power, and that in its nature easily adjusted, the more ready and appropriate mode would be an amendment in the ordinary form, on a proposition of two-thirds of both houses of Congress, to be ratified by three-fourths of the States: but, on the contrary, should the derangement of the system be great, embracing many points difficult to adjust, the States ought to be convened in a general convention, the most august of all assemblies, representing the united sovereignty of the confederated States, and having power and authority to correct every error, and to repair every dilapidation or injury, whether caused by time or accident, or the conflicting movements of the bodies, which compose the system.

" With institutions every way so fortunate, possessed of means so well calculated to prevent disorders, and so admirable to correct them, when they cannot be prevented, he, who would prescribe for our political disease, *disunion* on the one side, or *coercion of a State* in the assertion of its rights on the other, *would deserve* and *will receive the execrations of this and all future generations.*"

with contempt, as being either paid agents of Great Britain or crazy fanatics.

But here we have an illustration of the truth of M. Guizot's remark that some portions of history are without the control of human · judgment and will. Mr. Calhoun intended to arrest the Abolition agitation by appealing to the justice and reason of that portion, who were actuated by an honest zealotry, hoping thereby to withdraw them from the support of the *paid* emissaries of the British East-India cotton and sugar monopoly. His speech, however, had a directly contrary effect. By it he drew attention to the republicaniz-ing, levelling, democratizing influences of negro slavery, in its social and political effects upon the whites. By it he called attention to the peculiar influence of negro slavery in its bearing on the irrepressible conflict between capital and labor. By it, and by the cotemporary publication of M. de Cassagnac's book, Mr. Seward and Mr. Chase were brought to understand *why* the influence of the South was always exerted, in the legislation of the General Government, to keep up wages, and keep down the cost of living — in favor of light taxes, high wages, cheap living, and an economical administration of the Government. From Mr. Calhoun's speech and De Cassagnac's book the advocates of low wages learned that Abolition would produce pauperism; that pauperism would increase competition in the struggle for bread; that increased competition would reduce wages, with cheaper food and coarser clothing and fewer of the neces-saries of life to the laborers. The result was, not to detach the zealots from the British agents, but to bring the mon-archists, the aristocrats, the capitalists, and the advocates of low wages into an alliance with the British agents and the zealots; fusing them all, together with some other elements, into the great party, that elected Mr. Lincoln, made war upon and subjugated the South, and abolished slavery, that " free labor might be made cheaper than slave labor;" which simply means a reduction of the wages of free labor below the cost of feeding and clothing a negro and taking care of him in sickness and the infirmities of age.

We have referred to other elements in the fusion, that produced the party that elected Mr. Lincoln. The two *major* causes that led to that fusion and the consequent war, were unquestionably the conflict between despotic and free government; between the spirit of aristocracy and the spirit of democracy: and between capital and labor; the desire to make transitions to a monarchical and aristocratic government, and the desire to reduce wages. But there were other *minor* causes that deserve a passing notice.

And, first in importance, should be mentioned foreign intrigue to foster division between the North and the South, as shown in President Madison's message to Congress, with the accompanying correspondence of John Henry, the British emissary at Boston, to which the reader is referred.

In a letter from Boston, 20th March, 1809, to Sir James Craig, Governor-General of British America, John Henry said:

" It should, therefore, be the peculiar care of Great Britain to *foster division between the North and the South ;* and by succeeding in this, she may carry into effect her own projects in Europe, with a total disregard of the resentments of the democrats on this continent."

Unfortunately too many of the politicians of the United States have aided to make this British policy effective, " thus advancing (to use Mr. Guizot's language) in the execution of a plan, which they had not conceived, and of which they were not even aware."

One great statesman, unquestionably the ablest of his party now living, Mr. Seward, conceived the idea of governing this country by sectional animosities, as a permanent system. In a speech to the Maryland Legislature at Annapolis, shortly after the war, he suggested that, the sectional conflict between the North and South having been terminated, the time had arrived for a reorganization of parties, on the basis of a combination of the Eastern and Southern Atlantic States *against* the West.

Another of the minor causes of the war was the personal pique of disappointed aspirants for public office or patronage Among these the most notable were John Quincy Adams, Martin Van Buren, and Francis P. Blair.

Mr. Adams left the Federal party and joined the Democratic party, assigning, as his reason for so doing, that the former were traitors and disunionists ; but when the Democratic party rejected him as a candidate for the Presidency, he renewed his affiliation with his old party, and thereby gave color to the charge, made by some of the old Federalists, that his conversion to Democracy was pretended.   The bitterness of his subsequent hostility to the Democracy and to the South, their stronghold, leaves no room to doubt that his views were colored by the jaundice of disappointed ambition.

Mr. Van Buren, having been deserted by the Southern Democracy in his second race for the Presidency, took his revenge by the Free-soil Buffalo platform, and thereby gave an impulse to the fusion, which finally resulted in the election of Mr. Lincoln and the war.

Francis P. Blair had grown rich at Washington, as the editor of the Democratic newspaper, and by the public printing. Mr. Thomas Ritchie had grown old as a Democratic editor at Richmond, and was still poor.   On the election of Mr. Polk, the Virginia delegation in Congress, wishing to provide for Mr. Ritchie, urged that Mr. Blair had enjoyed the public patronage long enough, and ought to make room for Mr. Ritchie.   Mr. Polk admitted the force of the demand, and required Mr. Blair to sell out the Globe to Mr. Ritchie and General Armstrong of Nashville, who changed its name to the Union.   Mr. Blair yielded to superior force ; but held the South responsible for it.   He took his revenge by joining in the fusion that elected Mr. Lincoln and brought on the war;

aided greatly to break down the Democratic party; and only forgave and returned to his first love, when his revenge was full by the surrender to superior force at Appomattox Court House.(*a*)

Another of the minor causes that led to the war was the Pacific Railroad. That portion of the Democracy, who supported Breckinridge, were opposed to giving to a few individuals the enormous grants sought to be obtained from Congress in aid of that road, and had defeated the bill known as the Curtis Bill. Mr. Douglas himself, probably — certainly, Governor Herschel V. Johnson — and very many of those, who voted for them, were not aware of the plan, the execution of which was to be advanced by their nomination; but it was brought about by a *ring* of those, who expected to be the beneficiaries of some such Pacific Railroad Bill as that of Mr. Curtis; — to defeat Breckinridge, who would oppose it, and elect either Douglas or Lincoln, both of whom were pledged to its support. But, as it is my purpose to give a full history of the Pacific Railroad in another publication, I refer now to Duff Green's Facts and Suggestions, chap. xxvi., p. 215, for further information on this point.

In this connection, however, there was another remote, but very potent, cause of the war, that ought not to be passed unmentioned: the cession by the State of Virginia to the United States of her great territory northwest of the Ohio River. Mr. Calhoun doubtless had it in mind, when claiming for the South, among the other high qualities that adorn our nature, disinterestedness. Mr. Webster, in his speech in the Senate, March 7, 1850, said of it:

" And a most magnificent act it was. I never reflect upon it without a disposition to do honor and justice; — and justice would be the highest honor;—to Virginia, for the cession of her Northwestern territory. I will say, sir, it is one of her fairest claims to the respect and gratitude of the United States, and

(*a*) See note (*a*) to page xlii.

4

that, perhaps, it is only second to that other claim that
attaches to her ; that, from her counsels, and from the intelligence and patriotism of her leading statesmen, proceeded
the first idea put into practice of the formation of a general
Constitution for the United States. . . . I have said that I honor
Virginia for her cession of this territory.   There have been
received into the Treasury of the United States eighty millions of dollars, the proceeds of the sales of the public lands
ceded by her.   If the residue should be sold at the same
rate, the whole aggregate will exceed two hundred millions
of dollars."

In the light of more recent events, the historian may lose
sight of the disinterestedness and magnificence, in the prodi-
gality, of the gift ; for those, to whom she gave it, turned
upon and rent her in twain.   Nay, more ; while they heaped
honors on those, whose boast was that they desolated the
fair fields of Virginia, until a crow flying over them had to
"carry his rations with him," they sought to realize Mr. Calhoun's prophecy by putting the negro slaves, as political masters, over the sons of those, whose intelligence and patriotism
called forth these expressions of respect and gratitude from
Mr. Webster.

I remember to have seen, shortly after the war, the idea
advanced in a New York paper (I think the Journal of Commerce) that the South must thank her own statesmen and
leaders for her defeat ; because it was wholly due to that sentiment of love for the Union, which Southern statesmen had
striven so hard to arouse, and which Northern leaders had
striven with as much earnestness to suppress.

The proofs of this truth are multitudinous, but space admits
only the following extracts from the resolutions adopted at a
convention of the (so-called) Republican party of Massachusetts, at Worcester, not long previous to the war :

" Resolved, That the necessity for disunion is written in the
whole existing character and conditions of the two sections
of the country — in their social organization, education, habits,

and laws — in the dangers of our white citizens in Kansas, and of our colored ones in Boston — in the wounds of Charles Sumner and the laurels of his assailant — and no Government on earth was ever strong enough to hold together such opposing forces.

" Resolved, That this movement does not seek merely disunion, but the more perfect union of the free States by the *expulsion* of the slave States from the Confederation, in which they have ever been an element of discord, danger, and disgrace.

" Resolved, That henceforward, instead of regarding it as an objection to any system of policy, that it will lead to the separation of the States, we will proclaim that to be the highest of all recommendations and the grateful proof of statesmanship ; and will support, politically or otherwise, such men and measures as appear to tend most to this result.

" Resolved, That the sooner the separation takes place the more peaceful it will be ; but that peace or war is a secondary consideration in view of our present perils.   Slavery must be conquered, ' peaceably if we can, forcibly if we must.' " (*a*)

(*a*) For twenty years, from the time that Mr. Polk required him to give place to Messrs. Ritchie and Armstrong, in 1845, until Columbia was burned and Richmond evacuated, in 1865, Mr. Francis P. Blair more or less openly co-operated politically with the men, who passed these resolutions.   In a letter addressed, in 1855, to Daniel R. Goodloe and Lewis Clephane, Corresponding Committee of the Republican Association of Washington City, he assigned the reasons of his hostility to the Democratic party and to the South, as follows :

" The cause, which your organization is intended to promote, may well draw to its support men of all parties.   Differences on questions of policy, on constitutional construction, of modes of administration, may well be merged to unite men, who *believe* that nothing but concert of action on the part of those, who would arrest the spread of slavery, can resist the power of the combination now embodied to make it embrace the continent from ocean to ocean."

It is impossible for any one, who knows Mr. Blair, to believe that he *believed* what he here assigns as the reason of his combination with the men, who passed these resolutions.   He was too well informed, knew too much of geography, understood too well the climatic influences, which necessarily confined negro slavery to the Southern States, where alone it could be made profitable, to believe any such thing.   But as the close of a lady's letter is said to open the window of her heart, so the close of Mr. Blair's letter opens the window of his.   He said :

" Incumbents and expectants of office and dignities claim a sort of patent right

Here we have disunion avowed in Massachusetts, for the purpose of getting rid of the social and political influences of negro slavery. I have already shown that its social influence was to make the well-behaved poor white man the equal of his rich neighbor, and its political influence was exerted to secure light taxes, fair wages, and cheap living. Some of the party, like Mr. Greeley, were willing to "let the Union slide," if thereby they could be left free in the North and East to enjoy the distinctions between poor and rich, reduce wages, and tax labor and its products for the benefit of an aristocracy. But when the Union sentiment, created by Southern statesmen, showed itself, then the men, who passed these resolutions, were the loudest in crying "rebel," and in denouncing those, who took them at their word and proposed to separate peaceably. Then the monarchists, aristocrats, and advocates of low wages, previously avowed disunionists, endeavored to make, and did make, the "simple-hearted citizens," who loved the Union, believe that the South had begun the war. This was not true: for the first act of war was the military movement of Captain, now General, Robert Anderson, in taking possession of Fort Sumter; unless, perhaps, it would be more correct to say, that the first act of war was done by the men, who passed at Worcester the resolutions above quoted, when they sent John Brown and his band to Harper's Ferry, to incite a servile insurrection in Virginia.

The dominant party of Massachusetts demanded disunion, "peacefully if they could, forcibly if they must." The South, in answer to this demand, offered to withdraw peace-

---

in the machine of Government, to create a Democracy adapted to their purposes. Their innovations in the machinery are contrivances to renew their privileges for new terms."

Mr. Blair had long been the incumbent of the very lucrative office of public printer, and was forced to give way for Mr. Ritchie and General Armstrong, at the instance of the Virginia delegation. His long "incumbency" made him feel that he had "a sort of patent-right" in the profits of that office, and that his removal was an "innovation" in the machinery contrived by the Democratic party and the South.

fully; tendered the olive-branch; sent commissioners to Washington to arrange the terms of peaceful separation. Secession was resorted to as a peaceful measure, to satisfy the dominant party at the North, who had demanded the "*expulsion*" of the South from the confederation. Some, as I have said, cared only to get rid of negro slavery; so that the North, relieved from its democratic tendencies, might more readily make transitions to a monarchical and aristocratic form of government, with high taxes, low wages, and large Government expenditures. Another class saw, in the larger expenditures of a war, the chance of making fortunes by contracting for army supplies; and their purpose to provoke a war was disclosed by the remark about "blood-letting," made by Senator Chandler, whose display of gorgeous liveries and other insignia of pretensions to nobility, on his tour through Europe since the war, in some measure compensated newspaper men for the dearth of excitements when the war was over. But there was another class of men at the North, those, whom M. Guizot calls the "simple-hearted citizens," whom Southern statesmen had taught to love the Union, and who, full of courage and virtue, though little mindful of political affairs till something startling happens to arrest their attention, rose up to declare that the Union should be preserved. The South was willing — anxious — to remain in, and even after secession to return to, the Union, if permitted to do so with their rights inviolate under the Constitution. In December, 1860, President Buchanan despatched to Mr. Lincoln a gentleman, (*a*) a connection by marriage of the latter, to invite him to come to Washington at once; with assurances that he would be received as a guest at the White House, with all the honors due to him as President elect; and that

(*a*) This was my father, General Duff Green. Mr. Buchanan selected him to be the bearer of his invitation to Mr. Lincoln, supposing that through the marriage connection he would have more influence with Mr. Lincoln than almost any other messenger, who could have been selected. Ninian Edwards, of Springfield, Illinois, was my mother's nephew, and he and Mr. Lincoln had married sisters.

by uniting their influence, they could yet satisfy the South that they could remain in, or return to the union, with safety to their rights, and honor to their character; that thus the farther progress of secession could be arrested, and the States, that had already acted, be brought back. Mr. Lincoln declined to accept Mr. Buchanan's invitation without the approval of Mr. Ben Wade, of Ohio, and some others, who would not consent to it; and the result was that the blood-letting and contracting portion of the aristocratic party carried their point, and succeeded in provoking the war.

A great effort was subsequently made to produce the impression at the North that the war was "the slaveholders' rebellion." Nothing could be farther from the truth. The slaveholders, with rare exceptions, were averse to war, and opposed to secession, lest it might lead to war. Only a few, very few, slaveholders, (who were misled into believing the Worcester declaration that the sooner the separation took place, the more peaceful it would be,) favored the movement. Let the candid reader bear in mind that property-holders are proverbially timid and averse to all political movements calculated to endanger property; and that the slaveholders had multiplied reasons for caution, in the peculiar nature of their property, which had legs and a will of its own to take itself off.

It is generally, but erroneously, believed at the North that Yancey, Rhett, Toombs, Benjamin, and some others, were the chief agents in bringing about secession. Their influence, however, was small, compared to that of Governor Joseph E. Brown, of Georgia; and for the reason that their arguments; — (such, for instance, as the offer to "drink all the blood that was spilled," attributed, truly or falsely, to Mr. Toombs;)—were intended to prove that secession would be peaceable, and were addressed to the slaveholders, who were in a minority of one to fifteen; while Governor Brown addressed himself to the non-slaveholders, who were a vast majority, as the census of

1860 will show. (*a*) Governor Brown was born in South Carolina, a self-made man, sprung from the non-slaveholding class of poor whites; and his influence with that class, who were proud of his talents and success, was not much less in South Carolina than in Georgia.

While Governor of Georgia before the war, he issued several papers addressed to the non-slaveholders, advocating secession with great adroitness and ability. His argument was in substance as follows:

That the (so-called) Republican party was coming into power, pledged and determined to abolish slavery, and to make the negro the equal of the poor white man.

That, inasmuch as slaves were property, and private property could not be taken without just compensation, the first result would be to tax the non-slaveholding mechanics, small farmers, croppers, and others of their class, to pay for the slaves.

That another result would be to reduce wages by the competition of the freed negro, who would make up by petty larceny for lower wages; that this would fall upon the laboring whites; because the slave-owners also owned the lands and the bank and railroad stocks, and could still provide for their

(*a*) The vast preponderance of the non-slaveholders appears by the following tabular statement, taken from the census of 1860. (See volume of Population, pp. 592 and 593, and volume of Agriculture, pp. 223 to 245.)

	Slaveholders.	White population.	Ratio of slaveholders to white population.
Alabama	33,730	526,271	1 in 15
Arkansas	11,481	324,143	1 " 28
Florida	5,152	77,747	1 " 15
Georgia	41,084	591,550	1 " 14
Louisiana	22,033	357,456	1 " 16
Mississippi	30,943	353,899	1 " 11
North Carolina	34,658	629,942	1 " 18
South Carolina	26,701	291,300	1 " 11
Tennessee	36,844	826,722	1 " 22
Texas	21,878	420,891	1 " 20
Virginia	52,128	1,047,249	1 " 19

children without labor; while the non-slaveholders would be further impoverished by taxation to pay for the slaves; and that it would be they — the non-slaveholders and their children — who alone would have to compete with the negroes for employment.

That another result would be to degrade their social position; because the freed negroes would not attempt to intrude into the well-furnished drawing-rooms of their late masters, but would force their way to the humble firesides of the poor mechanic and laborer, and insult them by demanding their daughters in marriage. (a)

By such arguments as these Governor Brown "fired the hearts" of the vast non-slaveholding majority, and by their votes swept the reluctant slaveholders into secession. When at a later period it was proposed by General Lee and others to put negroes into the army, it was the non-slaveholders, who most bitterly opposed it; because they shrank from a contact, which they feared would bring them down to a level with the negroes.

The war was not a slaveholders' rebellion. Notwithstanding the declaration passed by Congress, at the instance of the late President Johnson, that the only object of the war was to preserve the Union — though very few on either side conceived, or were even aware of, the plan, the execution of which they were advancing — it was fought on the one side — by those, who controlled the Government, and in whose minds the design of the vast machine was centred,— in the interest of monarchism and of the capital, that employs free labor; to destroy negro slavery; because its tendencies were anti-mon-

(a) It is due to Governor Brown to add that, as Chief Justice of the Supreme Court of Georgia, since the war, he has sought to shield the poor whites of that State from one degradation, by the fear of which he sought to " fire their hearts," when advocating secession, by deciding that the intermarriage of whites and negroes is prohibited. (See his opinion in the case of Charlotte Scott, plaintiff, vs. The State of Georgia, which those, who have not access to the Georgia Reports, will find in McPherson's Handbook of Politics for 1870, p. 474.)

archical, and its influence exerted in legislation to maintain the price of labor and cheapen the cost of living. On the other side, it was fought by the Southern non-slaveholders to avert pauperization by taxation, reduction of wages, and social debasement.

The great majority of the brave men, who did the hard fighting of the war, fought and bled and died, to keep the Southern States in the Union; yet their "judgment and will" were subordinated to the control of the men, who, in the Worcester resolutions, declared their purpose to be "the expulsion of the Southern States from the confederation."

Many conscientious men thought they were fighting to secure justice and liberty for the negroes; yet their "judgment and will" were subordinated to the control of men, who seized the first moment of power to oppress the negroes, by an unjust and unconstitutional tax upon the product of negro labor, cotton, while seeking to use the negroes as voting-machines, to oppress free white labor at the North by similar unjust and pauperizing taxation.

Mr. Attorney-General Akerman, in his speech in Representatives' Hall, Atlanta, Georgia, 1st September, 1870, sought to impress upon Southern capital the fact, that emancipation was a decree of *divorce* of its interests from those of labor.

He, or whoever prepared his speech for him, was aware, however, that this was a "serious topic." He therefore endeavored in that speech to ride on both sides of the "serious topic," by adding that, "looking at the white population alone, the cry of a conflict between labor and capital has generally been the cry of the demagogue, for the reason that capital has seldom been organized against labor; and labor has seldom, except in the small way of trades' unions, been organized against capital."

But what are the historical facts?

The following is an extract from a late report of the Massachusetts Bureau of Labor Statistics:

"BOSTON AND THE WORKING-WOMEN — A PITIABLE PICTURE.

Extract from the last Report of the Massachusetts Bureau of Labor Statistics.

"In Boston, a large proportion are workers in shops. We will take one trade, that of tailoresses and cloakmakers: they go to their work at seven, almost always without any warm breakfast; they work till ten, and then perhaps have a few minutes' rest, when the little teapot is set on the range and a lunch of dry food eaten; but in most of the establishments the girls do not stop work till twelve, when, in all, they are allowed from thirty to sixty minutes for dinner. Work ends at five P. M., and many of the girls take work home with them, work not ceasing till midnight. Room-rent costs not less than two dollars to three dollars each, with often two or more double beds in a room. In good shops and with brisk work they can earn a dollar a day. Some machine girls receive more, but the work is very wearing, and induces spinal disease. One of our largest as well as kindest custom-work merchant tailors testified to a committee of inquiry, that few 'machine girls' could work over two years before becoming so broken down that they were ever after unfit for labor. In slopwork shops, girls can seldom earn more than their room-rent except by overwork. In slack times their suffering is extreme, girls having been known to work weeks with only water and bread or crackers for food, and fortunate if able to procure an ounce of tea. In dull times many have lived for weeks on five cents' worth each of stale bread per week while seeking work. The lodging-house keepers charge working-women higher rates than men, and many refuse to have them in their houses at any price. Hence they are often obliged to live and sleep in localities, where they would be ashamed to let any one know they ever went. Yet few ever break down morally or become untidy in dress. Those women, who take work home from the slopshops, provident, aid, and other charitable societies, receive as follows: Shirts, 4 cents to 7 cents; fine-bosomed shirts, 10 cents to 25 cents; satin vests, 20 cents; pants, 15 cents, 20 cents, and 37 cents; coats, 50 cents; French calico suits, lined sacks, faced skirt, 20 cents; long white night-dresses, 50 cents. Of the 30,000 women in and about Boston, who live by sewing, very few earn over $12 a week; the average wages do not exceed $2.75. Many poor women take this slop and charity work in quantities, and give it to others to do, still further lessening the receipts of the actual workers, who are usually women with small families dependent upon their labor for support. Paper-box makers average about $3 per week.

"Factory life is much harder on women than it was twenty-five years ago. Instead of tending two looms, as then, she is required to tend six; while a week's work now will not procure as much comfort as when she only tended one loom. Very few working-women of any class ever have a good bed, with sufficient bed-covering. Their wages will not allow them to purchase warm flannel undergarments or serviceable shoes, water-proofs, etc. Few are ever exempt from diseases caused by scanty clothing, insufficient and in-nutritious food, and long-continued labor in deleterious con-ditions. The constant pressure of anxiety breaks down many girls physically, and too often morally, before they reach the prime of life. All avenues of employment are overcrowded."

The New York Times, under Mr. Raymond's management, was, and still is, one of the ablest exponents of the doctrine that "free labor is cheaper than slave labor." On the 14th July, 1868, it said editorially:

"The New Orleans Commercial Bulletin says that the Southern planters, 'profiting by free labor, have now discov-ered that more money can be made out of a freedman's labor than from that of a slave.' We are glad to hear it. In the old days of slavery, we always told the Southern people that this was the case."

On the 21st July, 1869, the New York Times spoke editorially of the great Asiatic slave-trader of the nineteenth century, Koopmanschap, as follows

"It was only a few weeks ago that the name of Koopmanschap was unknown to fame. Suddenly it has emerged from the obscurity, with which the appellations of ordinary mortals are surrounded, and *occupies a lofty niche within the nation's fame.* Everybody is asking 'Who is Koopmanschap?' Fortunately he has arrived in the city just in time to answer for himself this question, as propounded to him by our reporter yesterday."

Now why does this advocate of cheap labor and dear living give such *a lofty niche in the nation's fame* to this trader in human bones and flesh and muscle? Is there, can there be, any other reason than because this new organization of the labor system of the United States proposes to furnish capital with cheaper labor, giving to capital all the advantages of the slave system, and at the same time relieving capital from the expense and burden of taking care of labor in sickness and the infirmities of age? Oh, admirable, money-making philanthropy!

But let the New York Times speak for itself. It says: "It is the importation of these coolies in the past, and the proposed transportation immediately of hundreds of thousands more, to supply the demand for labor everywhere, and in every industrial department, and especially to cultivate the neglected plantations of the South, that have *made the name of Koopmanschap famous* in the land.

". . . The woollen factory of Lazar frères, in San Francisco, employs 300 Chinamen, who make splendid hands, although they were entirely ignorant of the business when first employed by that firm. This was two years ago, when the Irish hands refused to work more than eight hours a day. The firm immediately discharged them, and employed the coolies, paying the latter for ten hours' labor a day only $1 per diem on an average, while to the Irish laborers they had paid on an average $3 per diem, or from $60 to $100 per month. . . .

"Mr. Koopmanschap says that he does not bring over Chinese women. They are sure to follow wherever the men go. The Chinamen will import them for themselves."

The Cincinnati Commercial is another noted advocate of these politico-economical ideas. It also sings pæans to Koopmanschap, and revels in the thought of a coming millennium of cheap labor. It says:

"Weavers of cotton and silk can be had in China for two or three dollars a month, and skilled artisans receive from five to eight dollars for that period of time. . . .

"Women are found in abundance in China to do the labor of households for their mere bread and clothing. Laborers can be got in the tea districts of China for six or seven cents a day. . . .

"The American laborer consumes enough meat, tea, and coffee, two or three times a day, to keep a Chinaman for a week. The price of meat, as is well known, is about four or five times that of bread. . . .

"The subsistence of the great mass of the Chinese is extremely simple. The great staple, of which it consists, is rice, and this, mixed with a little bread, a few vegetables, a little fruit, and a little meat, (more frequently fish,) constitutes the whole diet of millions. Indeed, the small consumption of animal food in China is one of the wonders of the country to a stranger. The flesh of beef or mutton is scarcely ever tasted except by the rich, and no Chinese ever use either milk, butter, or cheese."

Such is the Barmecide feast to which the so-called Republicanism of 1871 invites the laboring and productive classes of America.

On the other hand, the question of cheap labor and cheap production, which are the great problems of the age, has been so well treated by Ex-Governor Horatio Seymour, in a recent address to a mass meeting of working-men in Utica, New York, that I here insert it entire.

SPEECH OF EX-GOVERNOR SEYMOUR.

At a mass meeting of working-men in Utica, New York, Ex-Governor Seymour spoke as follows :

"At the last six annual elections in this State the Republican leaders have asked that they should be kept in power, because they claimed they had saved the country, and we are left to the conclusion that they saved it for their own special benefit. We do not see the grounds for this claim, so far as the war is concerned, as we sent our full share of men to the field. The city of New York, the stronghold of the Democracy, did more than its share in filling the ranks of our armies. If we look at the action of the party in power, the question comes up, what kind of salvation have they given us ? Our whole people are grievously burdened by taxation. Military power still tramples upon the judiciary in many parts of the South, and even threatens the sanctity of the ballot-box at the North. Great armies are kept up upon the pretext that they are needed to save the negroes at the South, and to kill the Indians at the West. The country is harassed by Indian and African problems. It is now also perplexed with the Asiatic question. It comes up like a black cloud upon our Western borders, taking unusual forms and proportions. To all, who have studied it, it causes great anxiety. Its shadows fall upon us, and we cannot get rid of its dangers by shutting our eyes to its evil forebodings. It enters into this election, for we are about to choose our lawmakers, who must deal with it. Some months ago I wrote a short letter in answer to an invitation from a body of working-men to speak to them upon this subject. I took ground not only against the way, in which the Chinamen come to our country, but to their coming here at all. That letter was sharply censured, but it was not written without thought or study. As the subject is fairly up in this canvass, I will speak of it to-night. Heretofore, except at the time when the people of New York and New England were bringing negroes from Africa to sell ·to the people of the South, immigration has always brought us people kindred to ourselves in manners, customs, and religion. Even their languages had much in common. The literature of Europe, translated into different tongues, was more or less known to them all. They had the same habits of thought, and were used to the same form of civilization. Their coming gave no shock to our institutions, laws, or habits. They rapidly became part of ourselves, and added to the general wealth and prosperity. Europe was not so overcrowded with people that they were sent to us in great numbers, or more rapidly than they could be assimilated. We therefore welcomed them to our shores. The Chinese immigration is a different thing. It comes from a land crowded with people beyond what our civilization could tolerate. They outnumber us ten to one. It brings to us a people who are in conflict with all our methods of thought, with all our ideas of morals, and with all our conceptions of government. While we find much to commend in their industry, there is more to condemn in their cunning, their cruelty, and in that stolidity of character, which makes them unimpressible by any influences we can bring to bear upon them. They will always be an undigested, hurtful thing in our political system. The idea prevails that they are a docile, harmless race; and so they are while they remain a few individuals scattered through the community. But study their characters at home, and you will find thieving, corruption, and falsehood in the interior of the state, piracy upon its coasts, and robbery upon its inland borders.

"They are hated by all other Asiatics. While some urge that we should welcome them here, they are debating the question if they shall go on with the massacre of Americans and Europeans, which they began with the awful slaughter of the men and women, who are engaged among them, as missionaries, in works of charity and religion.   Unfortunately for our country, our difficulties in dealing with this question are increased by the late amendments to the National Constitution, which have stripped the States of rights needed for their good government.   Otherwise this question could have been left to the Pacific States, who would have dealt with it in the light of their own experience.   But the Fifteenth Amendment binds California and Oregon hand and foot, and lays them prostrate before the Chinaman, who strides over them, and we are forced to confront him here.   It is urged by some that Chinese immigration will lower the wages of our labor, cheapen production, and add to the national wealth.   This is not true.   Cheap labor does not add to a nation's wealth, neither does it cheapen production, as I will show.   Look over the map of the world, and you will find universal poverty where labor is most poorly paid.   In Africa, you can buy a man's labor for life for a string of beads, but they are too poor to get the string of beads.   In Asia, the laborer gets a little better pay; but how little is its wealth, and how small is its commerce, compared with its countless millions of people! Men, who wear scanty cotton clothing, cannot uphold arts or industry.   They cannot give life and prosperity to the workshop, to the counting-house, or to fleets of vessels upon the ocean.   If you compare Asia and Africa with Europe, you will find that, while the laborers of England, of Germany, of France, and other countries are much better paid, the national wealth is greater, and that they are sending their products to the very regions where the pay of labor is at the lowest ebb. The labor of Europe, whose wages are so much higher than those of the other continents I have named, can still produce all the products of art for a much less price, and can and does sell them to those countries, where labor starves for want of pay. But we must turn to our own country to learn how true it is that labor must be well paid to give wealth and prosperity to a land. If the laborers and mechanics of the United States were put upon the same pay given to the Chinamen, we should have universal bankruptcy throughout the bounds of our country. Three-quarters of the stores of this city would be closed. Why is it that a town with 10,000 people here does more business than a city of 100,000 in Asia? It is due to the fact that our mechanics are able to build houses; to furnish them with the comforts of life; to clothe themselves and their families, not only in a way which protects their persons, but also gratifies their tastes; which enables them to support the arts and industry in all its forms. Why are the people of these United States able to pay a percentage of taxation, which would crush any other nation? It is simply because the wages of labor here enable men to consume all those varied articles, which pay a duty to Government. Go where you will, the world over, and you will find the greatest general wealth, the greatest prosperity, and the greatest happiness, where you find the greatest wages for labor. Men confound cheap labor with cheap production. These are not only different, but at times they are opposite things. Sometimes cheap labor is an element in cheap production, but that is not the rule. We see the fact to be that, where labor is the highest, production is the cheapest, and sends its works of art and of skill all over the world. The reason of this is, cheap production is the result of intellect as well as labor; of mind as well as of toil. It is wrought out by those, who are in that condition of comfort and respectability, that their minds are educated and alert. Starving labor never yet invented machinery to till the ground and gather in its crops; it never yet worked out those wonders in mechanics, which have borne our country on to its greatness. Men can cheapen their productions and add to their earnings when they can call to their aid science and learning, but

5

these two cannot live where labor is pinched down to the point of starvation. If man invents a machine, which enables him to make more, he can yet sell for less and grow rich. But force him to sell for less by the competition of the Chinaman, which does not increase his power of production, and he starves. And when the laborer sinks, the whole structure of society, of which he is the basis, sinks with him. This may be laid down as a law — that cheap production and general prosperity are the results of high civilization and general intelligence; that these can only exist among a people, where the great mass of the working men are well paid and placed in the condition of respectability, where their minds are fed as well as their bodies. But it is said there is no danger that the Chinamen will come to this country in such numbers as will harm our working-men. Is this true? We find that the character and condition of the Chinese is such that they can be sent for as readily as so many boxes of tea. We learn every day of orders that are sent out for thousands of them for special purposes. Orders are now under way for bands of them to make boots and shoes. It does not take a large number, thrown into this branch of business, to overstock the demand for this labor, and to unsettle the wages of those, who are skilled in this business. Already the artisans engaged in this trade are uneasy. They do not know how soon that skill, which they have gained in it, may be made valueless to support their families in the condition they have heretofore lived. The men who make clothes or hats, or other classes of our mechanics, may be treated in the same way. Those, who work in our factories, are liable to be driven out by orders, which are even now on their way to Asia. Navigation on the Pacific, as its name implies, has always been less costly and dangerous than that of the stormy Atlantic. There are now about one hundred and fifty thousand Chinamen in our country. An equal number, brought here by selfish and designing men, may be so placed as to force down the wages of working-men. The mere fact, that this can be done, destroys the independence and clouds the hopes of the body of our mechanics. There is a growing belief in men's minds that the mission of Mr. Burlingame was contrived by a class of manufacturers to effect this very object, at the moment they were appealing to Congress for special legislation in their own behalf. Short-sightedness is always incident to selfishness and greed. Let these men bear in mind that, when they have broken down the body of the laborers of this country, they will have destroyed their ability to be the consumers of manufactured products. The evils of underpaid labor will not fall upon the working-men alone. All classes must suffer when they are made poor. The owners of real estate, the merchant, the manufacturer, will find that the laws of trade and the rules of value are universal and unvarying. They will operate in Europe or America, as they do in Asia or Africa. True statesmanship and generous wisdom ever look to building up the interests of labor. Where the homes of toil are happy, and where prosperity waits upon the hand of industry, there is national greatness, wealth, and glory. But we are asked, What can we do to avert these evils? How can we hinder the landing upon our shores of swarms of Asiatics, without overturning the established maxim as to immigration? We need no change of our policy in this respect. We put the Asiatic and the European upon the same footing. Our laws have never allowed any nation to send here a hurtful or a dangerous class of men. When in some instances they have shipped paupers to our shores, we have sent them back. We forbid the violators of laws, men who endanger the public health or order, to land here. The statutes of the different States and of the nation are full of such regulations. We welcome the great body of European immigrants, because it is for our advantage to have them here. The Chinaman has no better rights than the German, the Irishman, the Englishman, or the Frenchman. If his coming here is hurtful to the good order of society, to the great interests of industry, we have a right to keep him away. If there is danger that they will pour into the Pacific States in such numbers as to shape their customs and habits by Asiatic rules, then they endanger our Union, for the end of this must be their utter severance from the rest of our country. The Mormons are not so much in conflict with our ideas of morals and civilization as are the Chinese. Yet no one would tolerate the idea that the Mormons should gain control of the Pacific coast. This Government is even now adopting sharp measures to hold them in check, at their colony in the midst of the great deserts of the West. A simple law, such as has been adopted with regard to foreign immigration, will settle this whole question. Let Congress declare that no more than ten Chinamen shall be landed from one vessel, and they will close to a safe degree those floodgates, which are now wide open, and through which we are threatened with an invasion from Asia as hurtful as that, which once desolated Europe under Genghis Khan. I have spoken thus plainly upon this subject, because I believe it more deeply concerns the welfare of the American people than any topic involved in this election. I have no censures for those who may differ from the views I hold. I have no prejudices, which will hinder me from changing those views, if I find that I am wrong. What I have said is the result of much thought and careful study. I wish that those, who are charged with the conduct of national affairs, or that their supporters, who are active in this canvass, had in a plain and open way stated their views with regard to this great Asiatic problem. I think that, by so doing, they would stand in a better light before the country and the world, than by efforts to keep alive sectional hate and partisan malice."

To the editorial comments of the New York Times on the fact noticed by the New Orleans Commercial Bulletin, it is only necessary to add one single example, out of millions, to illustrate that the effect of emancipation has already been to reduce wages, and to diminish the share of the products of labor, allotted to those, by whose labor they were produced. A negro woman, who was an excellent cook, was, by the casualties of the war, separated from her owners in 1864. In January, 1870, she was most happy to get back to them. She told them she had been doing her best to support herself, but had not been able to get more than her food and forty dollars a year, out of which she had to clothe herself, and pay for medicine and medical attendance. Before the war she could be hired readily for $125 to $150 per annum, with food, clothing, medicines, and medical attendance in addition.

Yet the Republican cry is still for cheaper labor! and Senator Sprague attended the Memphis Commercial Convention for the sole purpose of impressing on the mind of Southern capital that, having been *divorced* by emancipation from labor, it should now unite with Northern capital in measures to cheapen labor. (*a*)

In this *divorce* case, labor is the feebler party; — the poor deserted wife, left without alimony, and with a brood of hungry children crying for bread, and dependent on her for support!

Emancipation has taken from her that "natural ally," which a community of interests secured to her in the old days of negro slavery, as expressed in Mr. Jefferson's aphorism, above quoted. Wages no longer, at the South, go into, but they come out of, the pockets of capital. The cost of living, at the South, no longer comes out of, but goes into, the pockets of capital.

And now we have the authoritative declaration of the Attorney-General, the first law-officer of the Government, that Mrs. White Labor and Mrs. Black Labor are two lonely grass widows.

(*a*) See Senator Sprague's speech at the Memphis Commercial Convention.

The question arises, Where can they, in their lonesome grass - widowhood, turn for aid and comfort, food, and shelter?

Shall they "go to Chicago"? Alas, they are already *divorced by emancipation!* They would be glad to make an honest living, as hirelings, if they could get wages to keep soul and body together. But they shrink from living by beggary, prostitution, or theft. Then there is no use in their "*going to Chicago.*"

Shall they appeal to what is called *Republicanism* in 1871? Alas! with the old rakes of that set, who misled, deceived, and betrayed them, the heyday of the blood is over; their hearts are withered and callous! Besides, they brought about the *divorce*, of malice prepense, with set purpose to ruin these two poor women; that they might thereby be forced into one of De Cassagnac's four classes of the proletariat, viz., hirelings at cheap wages, or else beggars, prostitutes, or thieves!

Shall they appeal to the younger bloods of the set — any of the "smaller fry," who call themselves Republicans? Alas! they never had either hearts or brains; or, if they had, there was not phosphorus enough in their composition to light up the one, or warm the other! Besides, they belong, body and soul, to capital, and believe that, in the progress of civilization, the great need of the hour is *cheap labor!*

Can they find relief in what the Attorney-General calls "the small way of trades' unions"? Alas, alas, alas! our author shows that all history proves that to be a poor and vain reliance! Egotism, selfishness, appear there, as elsewhere. I attended the National Labor Convention in Baltimore in 1866, as a spectator, from curiosity, to see what it was composed of, and what were its objects. I was at the National Labor Convention in Chicago in 1867, as a delegate from the Pattern-makers' Union of Baltimore. I had not much to say at either Convention, but was a close observer at both. Of all the men, whom I saw at Baltimore or Chicago, only two impressed on me the idea that their purpose was to relieve the distress of the two poor *divorced* widows, Mrs. White Labor and Mrs. Black Labor. All the rest impressed me with the idea that their "judgment and will" were under the control of the few, in whose minds the designs of the machine were centred; or that egotism, selfishness, was their only motive; that their purpose was "to grind their own axes," and to get some control over the two poor lonesome grass widows, on which they could trade, for their own profit, with the advocates of cheap labor.

Can wan, pallid Mrs. White Labor find an asylum in the cabin of her dusky rival, Mrs. Black Labor, now the favored mistress of that wild *enfant perdu*, Imperialism, who is travelling, *incog.*, through the United States, under the assumed name of Republicanism?

Pshaw! Let Pharisees, who trade upon, and grow rich by, negrophilism, falsely prate about the equality or superiority of the negro over the white race, in all intellectual, moral, physical, social, and political aptitudes. Let charlatans in statesmanship vainly delude themselves with the belief, that, by such legislation as the Akerman Election Bill of Georgia, they can vote negroes, without challenge, as often as their party necessities require. Let would-be emperors fondly imagine that, because the *"colored troops fought nobly,"* the colored vote can be used to make them small Neros or Caligulas. All this is vanity and vexation of spirit. It is historically certain — at least I firmly believe — that thirty millions of the Caucasian race will not long consent to leave their destinies under the control of four millions of ignorant negroes, misled by bad white men, of very little more intellect than the negro, and with hearts blacker than the negro's skin.

Oh, that these poor divorced women could turn to some one of the noble and gallant men, whom they called "rebels," when in fact they were risking life and fortune, and lost everything but honor, for their sakes and in their cause! I could speak to them of men, whose names are synonyms for all that is great in intellect, noble in conduct, pure in morals, knightly in courtesy. I could point to one in Georgia, a native Georgian; brave as Marshal Ney, eagle-eyed and skilful as the first Napoleon, devout and sincere as Havelock or Robert E. Lee, the great Christian soldier, Major-General John B. Gordon, who was on the battle-field and in the Episcopal Church, what Stonewall Jackson was on the battle-field and in the Presbyterian Church. Near to him, in South Carolina, I could point to General William S. Walker, a Pennsylvanian by birth, but, like Gordon, "sans peur et sans reproche;" one who never deceived man or misled woman. I might name others. But, alas! all these men were Southern rebels. They fought bravely and conscientiously in a cause they believed to be right; yet, they were conquered — subjugated. Now they are prostrate. The dusky mistress of Imperialism has her pearl-embroidered slipper (*a*) on their necks.

Is there, then, no hope for the widows — is there no help for the widows' sons and daughters?

Yes. In the Democracy of the Great West, there yet remain traces of the pure republicanism of Jefferson and Madison, of Calhoun and Webster. There labor can find statesmen, who have never bowed the knee to Baal or to Mammon, nor accepted the idea that, in the progress of civilization, the great objects of social and political science are to cheapen labor, and to regulate the diet of American working men and women by the smallest quantities of rice and fish, on which an Asiatic can exist.

The first great need of labor is an honest and economical administration of Government. Prodigal expenditures require oppressive taxation, which, however disguised by the subtle and artful contrivances of modern legislation, labor and the products of labor in the end have to pay. (*b*)

(*a*) See chap. xvii.
(*b*) See chap. xiv., on the Fall of the Ancient Trades' Unions.

But what, more than all else, oppresses labor, and all, who employ labor in the pursuits of productive industry, is the subtle and artful fiscal contrivance, by which the control of the money of the country is centred in a few hands, enabling them by combination and concert of action to raise or lower the prices of the products of labor at pleasure, by making money scarce when they wish to buy, and abundant when they wish to sell. "Never," said Mr. Calhoun in the Senate, October 3, 1837 — "Never was an engine invented better calculated to place the destiny of the many in the hands of the few, or less favorable to that equality and independence, which lie at the bottom of our free institutions."

I wish here to repeat, what I have said in my dedication, that under the designation of "The Laboring and Burgher Classes of America," I include all of the learned professions — all, who labor with the brain or with the hand — all, who wish to live and grow rich by the fruits of their own honest industry — all, who do not seek to live by plundering the Federal or State treasuries, nor by Congressional or State class legislation.

What they all require is an abundant and cheap measure of prices, of uniform and stable value.

But a further discussion of this subject would make this preface too long, and I propose to treat of it in another book.

If I have succeeded in dispelling some few of the many errors, under which the Northern and Western mind have been befogged, in reference to the causes and results of the late Civil War in America, my present purpose will have been accomplished.

BEN. E. GREEN.

HOPEWELL, near Dalton,
 Whitfield County, Georgia,
  February, 1871.

POSTSCRIPT.

W E have already alluded briefly (see p. xlviii.) to the repugnance of the non-slaveholding whites of the South to the
proposition for negro enlistments in the Confederate armies; a
repugnance which even the great name and magic influence of
Robert E. Lee could not overcome. This proposition was advocated by General Lee at a late period of the civil war — perhaps too
late to have changed the results. Reluctant as we are to detain our
readers, we would feel that our part of this work was incomplete if
we failed to notice the fact, that long before General Lee came to
that conclusion, there was one man whose forecast anticipated that
some such measure would be indispensable to the success of the
Confederate cause. That man was Colonel John T. Pickett, who
was selected, on account of his previous Mexican experience, as
the first diplomatic agent of the Confederate States in Mexico.
Early in the war — under date of Vera Cruz, February 22, 1862 —
he submitted, for the consideration of the Confederate Government,
the following

"MEMORANDUM.

"Is there no mode by which we may be able to neutralize the
hostility existing throughout the world against our institution of domestic servitude? It is in vain to attempt to correct the gross mis-
apprehensions prevailing with regard to it. The word 'slavery' is
sufficient to condemn it among the peoples. Can we not invent a
better and more appropriate name for it? It is not 'slavery' as
understood among men; but we bear the odium as though it were.
The enactment of laws which would prohibit the separation of
mothers and children, (though what white family is not so separated?) the granting to the negroes certain civil rights, (so to speak,)

22   329

— such as protection from cruel and arbitrary punishment, right to change their masters if maltreated, privilege to purchase their freedom, etc., etc.,— might go far toward the end so much to be desired. Practically, these things do exist to a certain extent. The force of public opinion is protection to the negro, not to speak of the interest and even affection of the master. But the world at large knows not these things, and cannot or will not be convinced ; whereas, an expression of the supreme legislative will would appeal to the governments and to the enlightenment of the age. I resided for years in the British West Indies, made many visits to Hayti and to the Dominican Republic, have seen only too much of the fruits of indiscriminate equality among the mongrels and hybrids of Spanish America, and therefore no one can entertain sounder views on the great domestic question than I do. In short, emancipation *without* deportation would be national suicide ; *with* it, a chimera.''

These suggestions were not acted on for two reasons : first, because the question was a *local* one, belonging exclusively to the States, and the Confederate authorities had no constitutional power to touch it in any way ; secondly, because their whole time, attention, thoughts, and energies were absorbed in the question of *defence* — of repelling the armed invasion of their territory.

Colonel Pickett's idea was, that the inauguration of a scheme of gradual emancipation would emasculate the Abolition party of the North, satisfy Europe, and secure intervention, peace, and independence ; and that although the Constitution of the Confederate States gave to the Confederate Government no right to interfere with the local institutions of the States, yet the Confederate Congress might, by joint resolution, recommend some such action to the State Legislatures, and justify their recommendation by the plea of " *military necessity*,'' which in time of war covers, like charity at all times, a multitude of sins.

Colonel Pickett soon found that he could accomplish nothing by remaining in Mexico, and, without waiting for instructions from his Government, returned to take part in the active service of the field, as chief of staff to General Breckinridge. As Mr. Colwell, under the excitements of the war, came to the conclusion that negro slavery should be sacrificed to save the Union, so Colonel Pickett, from his standpoint, under the influence of his associations with the diplomatic representatives of the monarchies and empires of Europe, came to the conclusion that *the institution* should be sacrificed to secure European intervention, peace, and independence.

Subsequently, he ran as a candidate for the Confederate Congress, against General Humphrey Marshall, that he might officially and more effectually ventilate his views in favor of negro enlistments and gradual emancipation. He was defeated, not, as he supposes, by any intrigues of General Marshall, but because it got bruited about among the non-slaveholding whites that he was in favor of negro enlistments and gradual emancipation.

Still later, he learned that the Confederate Government contemplated sending another minister to Mexico, and, for the benefit of his successor in that mission, submitted the suggestions of his experience, as follows:

"The cause of Mexican hate toward us, as individuals and as a nation, is patent. . . . It may be said to arise, firstly, from the great aversion of the Mexicans to negro slavery; and, secondly, from jealousy of race, the natural dread a weaker people have for a stronger neighbor, and from the artfully contrived teachings of the United States Government as to past and future aggressions upon Mexican territory.

"As to the first proposition. It is impossible to unteach the Mexican mind on the subject of slavery. We daily feel what an abolition propaganda has done among a more enlightened people. But it ought to be in our power to persuade Mexican statesmen (for it will be with Mexicans that our diplomatist will have to deal, even under the government of Maximilian) that, although slavery has both its moral and political blessings, and as practised in the Confederate States, it is but a mode of hiring servants for life, while in other countries they are employed by the day, month, or year, yet we have never designed to force the institution upon our neighbor. It can be shown, too, that free colored people are regarded with more consideration and entitled to more substantial privileges among us, though not admitted to social and political equality, than in the United States. Our history will furnish instances. General Jackson treated the free colored inhabitants of New Orleans as 'citizens,' in a certain sense. We know that a large class in Mobile, of the present day, termed 'creoles,' are colored people, (whence the popular error as to the true signification of that word,) of French and Spanish admixture. It is also a fact that many adopted citizens of Texas have African blood in their veins. Neither did our Southerners in California object to the eminent Don Pio Pico because of his negro blood. But California, an Abolition State, refuses citizenship to the Chinese, (to which refusal the writer does not object, individually,) while, to my knowledge, some of the best families in Mexico have Chinese blood in their veins — the natural consequence of the annual galleon between Acapulco and Manilla. I was on very friendly terms with the head of one of these families, Don Luis Jauregui. But the most striking contrast of this whole picture would be the treatment which the negroes received from a New York mob not many months ago.

"It would be an ungracious office, but we might remind the Mexicans that they enslave their own race. Indeed, white *peons* are very numerous, and *peonage* is the most atrocious system ever conceived of. It is slavery for debt, without provision for infancy, sickness, or old age. It is transmitted from father to son, while with us the child takes the condition of the mother only. But hear Commodore Perry on the subject of Mexican peonage. 'God pity these poor creatures!' says the commodore in his journal, in reference to the laboring classes of the Lew Chew Islands. 'I have seen much of the world, have observed savage life in many of its conditions, but *never*, unless I may except the miserable *peons* of Mexico, have I looked upon such an amount of apparent wretchedness as these squalid slaves would seem to suffer.'

"It is a system which would have disgraced the laws of Draco, which are said to have been written in blood. If we were as-hypocritical and meddlesome as our Northern brethren, and were in a condition to do so, we might *cajole* the world by a *crusade* against this enslavement of white men. We might create a great sensation, too, by broaching a scheme for the amalgamation of the white and red races of the continent. Why should it not be as great an honor to claim the blood of Montezuma as that of Powhatan? At least, let us impress Mexicans with the fact that we have no prejudice against their native race — that Indians are citizens with us, and sit in our national legislature. It would be well, also, to explain to them that it is in the abolition programme to colonize Mexico with North American negroes of the Protestant (i. e. 'heretic') faith, and speaking the English language.

"As a proof that Mexico is thoroughly abolitionized, I will mention that, during my long residence as United States Consul at Vera Cruz, I never succeeded in reclaiming, by intervention of local authority, a single negro deserter from the vessels of my nation; while, on the other hand, I scarcely ever failed to have the white sailors returned promptly. I think the accomplished gentleman * mentioned in connection with the secretaryship of the new mission has some official knowledge of this fact. I will dismiss this part of my theme by suggesting that the envoy procure some of our standard Southern works on the slavery question. They may be useful to him, and cannot, probably, be procured in Mexico. He can easily obtain the published Northern view of the subject in that capital, and should do so. *Fas est ab hoste doceri*."

Colonel Pickett is an accomplished scholar, a sound thinker, a quick and acute observer. Yet the standpoint from which his observations were taken did not command a view of the whole field. He looked at the subject only as a diplomatist, intent on one object, viz. peace and independence through the instrumentality of an European intervention. Consequently, like M. Guizot, (see *ante*, p. 134,) with many clear and correct views, he stopped halfway on his road to a great discovery. He saw that the world is governed by *sensations;* but he did not prosecute his inquiries far enough to discover *who created* these *sensations*, and for what purposes. If he had done so, he would have seen that *self-interest* was at the bottom; that "man advances in the execution of a plan which he has not conceived, of which he is not even aware, and which he comprehends very imperfectly," while "its designs are centred in a single or in few minds."

He saw that the diplomatic representatives of European despotisms were bitterly and unchangeably opposed to the *peculiar institution of negro* slavery in the Southern States, while they had no word

* Walker Fearn, Esq., Secretary of Legation to Mexico with the Hon. John Forsyth, Minister Plenipotentiary.

of sympathy for the far more wretched condition of the *peons* of Mexico, nor for the slaves of the Lew Chew Islands and of the British East Indies.

He did not stop, or rather he did not go on, to inquire why this was so. If he had, he would have discovered that negro servitude, as it existed in the Southern States, being a *peculiar* institution, produced *peculiar* political and politico-economical results.

1st. Its tendency was to strengthen the democratic principle of political and social equality among the rich and poor whites.

2d. It elevated the whites, however poor they might be, above the degradation of selling their votes.

3d. It *married* capital to labor, by making it the interest of capital to keep up wages, which went into its pocket, and to keep down the cost of living, which came out of its pocket.

4th. The result of these *peculiar* influences was to give *stability* to *free* institutions, causing the Southern States to be "*constantly inclined most strongly to the side of liberty; the first to see and the first to resist the encroachments of power;* and, by the *marriage* of capital to labor, it enlisted capital on the side of labor against that legislative policy which seeks to cheapen labor, to increase taxes, and to squander the taxes paid by labor for the profit of capital." (See Calhoun's speech, *ante*, p. xxxii.)

If Colonel Pickett had pushed his observations beyond the diplomatic into the politico-economical field of inquiry, he would have discovered that, on the part of the advocates of centralism and of capital, emancipation was the chief object of the war; because,

1st. Emancipation would *divorce* Southern capital from labor;

2d. It would destroy the chief support of the democratic principle of equality among the whites, and place the Government on *the inclined plane* to monarchy;

3d. It would substitute for the *incorruptible* votes of the poor whites of the South the *cheaply purchasable* votes of negro freedmen, to neutralize the votes of the working and burgher classes of the North and West.

When Colonel Pickett said that "emancipation without deportation would be national suicide; with it, a chimera," he spoke of *immediate emancipation in mass.* His observations and experience in Mexico and the West Indies doubtless satisfied him, as ours did us, that *deportation* was surrounded with practical difficulties which made the scheme chimerical. Those difficulties were, first, the enormous expense of moving 4,000,000 of people, and of taking care of them *in transitu*, and until located in new homes; second, their inability to take care of themselves after they were located, as shown by the fate of the American negro colony on the island of Santo Domingo; third, the inhumanity of the "frightful misery" which must inevitably result from turning them off to take care of themselves; and, finally, because their labor was indispensable where they were, and could not be supplied except by a slow and gradual system, running through a long course of years.

This idea of gradual emancipation *with* deportation originated with Mr. Jefferson, fifty years ago — long before the very *peculiar* politico-economical results of the *peculiar institution* were analyzed by the master mind of Calhoun. Up to the close of the war, deportation of the negroes was a favorite idea with most of the prominent leaders of the *monarchical cheap-labor* party.

On the 8th of December, 1859, Senator Trumbull said :

" When we say that all men are created equal, we do not mean that every man in organized society has the same rights. We do not tolerate that in Illinois. I know that there is a distinction between these two races, because the Almighty himself has marked it upon their very faces; and, in my judgment, man *cannot, by legislation or otherwise*, produce a perfect equality between these races, so that they will live happily together. . . . I trust that an idea foreshadowed by Mr. Jefferson will hereafter become, although it is not now, part of the creed of the Republican party. I mean the idea of the deportation of the free negro population from this country. . . . It seems impracticable to transport this great population to Africa. Let us obtain a country nearer home; and I know I may say for the people whom I represent, we will contribute liberally of our means to relieve the country of the free negro population. I hope it may become the policy of the Republican party . . . to deliver the country from the only element which ever seriously threatened its peace, and furnish the means of relieving it from the evils of a large free negro population. By such a course we may lay the foundation for continued and permanent prosperity."

On the 13th of April, 1860, Senator John Sherman, in a speech at the Cooper Institute, New York, favored the idea of the "gradual colonization of the negro population of the United States in the Central American States," where they might be "free from the domination of the white race."

On the 7th of March, 1860, Senator Wade, of Ohio, said, in the Senate of the United States:

"This great Government owes it to various pressing considerations to provide a means whereby the free negroes may emigrate to some congenial clime, where they may be maintained to the mutual benefit of all. This would insure a *separation of the races.* Let them go into the tropics. There are vast tracts of most fertile and inviting lands, in a climate perfectly congenial to that class of men, where the negro will be predominant, where his nature seems to be improved, and all his faculties, both mental and physical, are fully developed, and where the white man degenerates in the same proportion as the black man prospers. Let them go there ; *let them be separated;* it is easy to do it. They will be so far removed from us that they cannot form a disturbing element in our *political economy.* . . . I hope, after that is done, to hear no more about negro equality, or anything of the kind. We shall be as glad to rid ourselves of these people as anybody else can."

On the 21st of August, 1858, at Ottawa, Ill., Mr. Lincoln said:

"I have no purpose to introduce political and social equality between the white and black races. There is a physical difference between the two, which, in my judgment, will probably *forever* forbid their living together upon the footing of perfect equality; and, inasmuch as it becomes a necessity that there must be a difference, I am in favor of the race to which I belong having the superior position."

In the course of his canvass with Mr. Douglas, in Illinois, in 1858, Mr. Lincoln repeatedly declared that he was opposed to "a social and political equality between the white and black races ; " that he "was not in favor of negro citizenship ; " and that he would "to the very last stand by the law of Illinois which forbade the marriage of white people with negroes." He also declared that, in his "opinion, it would be best for all concerned to have the colored population in a State by themselves."

Finally, in his messages to Congress and otherwise, Mr. Lincoln urgently advocated *gradual emancipation with deportation.*

In his annual message, December 3, 1861, he said :

" To carry out the plan of colonization may involve the acquiring of territory, and also the appropriation of money beyond that to be expended in the territorial acquisition. . . . If it be said that the only legitimate object of acquiring territory is to furnish homes for *white* men, this measure effects that object; for the *emigration of colored* men leaves *additional room for white* men remaining or coming here. Mr. Jefferson, however, placed the importance of procuring Louisiana more on *political* and commercial grounds than on providing room for population.

"On this whole proposition, including the appropriation of money with the acquisition of territory, does not the expediency amount to absolute necessity — that *without which the Government itself cannot be perpetuated ?*"

This amounts to an assertion by Mr. Lincoln that emancipation without deportation would be national suicide.

But why tear from their homes, and from the "kind, protecting care" they then enjoyed, 4,000,000 of negroes, to banish them to the "frightful misery" of taking care of themselves in the Central American States? Did any idea of good will for the negroes enter into this scheme for their banishment? Surely not; for when Mr. R. M. T. Hunter, at the Hampton Roads conference, alluded to the sufferings which would result to the old and infirm, and to the women and children, who were unable to support themselves, the only answer was the following story, told by Mr. Lincoln :

"'An Illinois farmer was congratulating himself with a neighbor upon a great discovery he had made, by which he could economize time and labor in gathering and taking care of the food crop for his hogs, as well as trouble in looking after and feeding them during the winter.

" 'What is it ?' said the neighbor.

" 'Why, it is,' said the farmer, ' to plant plenty of potatoes, and when they mature, without either digging or housing them, turn the hogs in the field, and let them get their own food as they want it.'

" 'But,' said the neighbor, 'how will that do when the winter comes, and the ground is hard frozen ?'

" 'Well,' said the farmer, *let 'em root!*' "

(See the War between the States, by A. H. Stephens, vol. ii., p. 615. Barrett's Life of Lincoln, p. 827.)

From the inhumanity of saying to the old and infirm negroes, and to the women and children who were unable to support themselves, "*Root, hog, or die*," the Southern people shrank with greater indignation than Plutarch felt for Cato. (See p. 275.) There was no trace of benevolence or pity for the negroes in that sentiment.

Did an overcrowded territory require that the negroes should be driven out, like the Indians, to make *additional room* for white men? It is true that Mr. Lincoln's message of December 3, 1861, gives prominence to this argument, and his message of December 1, 1862, elaborates the idea that the time is fast approaching when our population will have so increased, that, "*instead of receiving the foreign-born, as now, we shall be compelled to send part of the native-born (the negroes) away.*" To show when that time would probably arrive, Mr. Lincoln, or rather Mr. Seward, (for his handiwork is clearly perceptible in both messages,) said: " Several of our States are already above the average of Europe — 73¼ to a square mile. Massachusetts has 157, Rhode Island 133, Connecticut 99, etc., etc."

Then he gives a tabular statement of decennial increase, showing that in 1930 our population *may* reach the overcrowded number of 251,680,914; and concludes thus:

" These figures show that our country *may* be as populous as Europe now is, at some point between 1920 and 1930 — say about 1925 — our territory, at 73¼ persons to the square mile, being the capacity to contain 217,186,000."

Now, this argument of Mr. Seward, and his ingenious sophistries about capital and labor in the same messages, were as false and as deceptive as his dogma of the irrepressible conflict between free labor and slave labor. They were adroitly and ably prepared for the express purpose of misleading and enticing the working and burgher classes of the North into an indiscretion, a false step, against their natural ally and *politically-wedded spouse;* the consequence of which would be, and since has been, a declaration of the Attorney-General that labor is now a divorced grass-widow !

The so-miscalled Republican party were not acting in good faith with white labor when they endeavored, in 1861 and 1862, to make it appear that their purpose was to drive out the negroes to make additional room for the rapidly increasing white population. This is apparent from the fact that, since their object has been accomplished, by *divorcing* capital from labor by emancipation, we hear nothing more said about deporting the negroes. So far from being the special friends of the negroes, they were actuated by a malevolence to the negro almost as atrocious as Sherman's treatment of the women and children of the white working classes of Atlanta. This is apparent from the proposition to drive away the negroes from their comfortable homes, and say to their old and infirm and women and children, "*Root for yourselves, like hogs, or die!*"

Moreover, in the same message, in speaking of our vast territory of 2,963,000 square miles, Mr. Seward admits that they furnish abundant room, a broad national homestead, an ample resource against an overcrowded condition for at least fifty years to come — perhaps much longer. Then, why drive the poor negro away now, into the Central American States, to Santo Domingo, or elsewhere?

Mr. Seward, the Oily Gammon of politics, throws out a cautious intimation that, like Mr. Jefferson's acquisition of Louisiana, there was a *political* object to be gained. Bluff Ben Wade, in his bluff way, blurts out the true answer, and says, "*The negroes form a disturbing element in our* POLITICAL ECONOMY."

Why disturbing? We have already given the true answer, but it cannot be repeated too often. If Mr. Wade was candidly and confidentially explaining this *disturbance* to one of his party friends or followers, his language, substituting *dashes* for the oaths with which he sandwiches his discourse, would be about as follows:

"This — — peculiar institution, under which these — — negroes exist in this country, has — — peculiar results. — — —, it marries capital to labor. It makes the — — owners of negroes vote with the — — working-men in the North and West. — — they want to keep up wages, because wages go into their — — pockets. They legislate with a view to keep down the cost of living, because they have to feed and clothe and nurse and take care of the — — negroes, and that comes out of their pockets. And — —, they go in for what they call an honest and economical administration of the Government, and — — they oppose our little occasional appropriations of a few millions or so, with which to enrich our party friends; and — —, they whine about these paltry millions coming partly out of their own pockets and partly out of the pockets of the — — working and burgher classes of the North and West. But — — —, these — — owners of negroes treat — — poor white men as equals. Now, all these — — disturbances of our political economy grow out of this — — *marriage* of capital to labor in the South. We must *divorce* them. We must separate the white from the — — negro race. We must send the — — negroes off into the tropics. Then Southern capital will vote with Northern and Western capital, and we can, by subtle and artful fiscal contrivances of legislation, impose as many burdens on the — — working-men, and grant as many privileges to capital, and make as many and as large appropriations for the benefit of our party friends as we — — please. And if we can get *rid* of these — — negroes by sending them away into the tropics, we can get rid of the — — democratic notion of the — — slave power about the equality of white men, which this — — peculiar institution fosters.''

As we have said, there can be no doubt that Mr. Seward prepared those portions of Mr. Lincoln's annual messages of 1861 and 1862 relative to the deportation of the colored population. It is not to be supposed, however, that Mr. Lincoln would have sent those messages to Congress without the concurrence and approval of the other members of his cabinet. These were S. P. Chase, Simon Cameron, Gideon Welles, Caleb B. Smith, Edward Bates, and Edwin M. Stanton. Now, if Mr. Lincoln and these his cabinet officers, and Senators Trumbull, Wade, and Sherman are to be accepted as the authorized exponents of the principles and policy of the so-miscalled Republican party, we have, in these messages and in the speeches of those senators, an official declaration of a purpose to drive the colored population out of the country, to make more room for white population, accompanied with the suggestion that it was a *necessity, without which the Government itself could not be perpetuated!*

Let the colored population bear this always in mind!!

Let the white population of the North and West bear in mind that since then the so-miscalled Republican party have taken a new departure!!!

Now, instead of "sending the negro population into the Central American States, where they may be free from the domination of the white race," they have subjected the white race in the South to the domination of the negro. Why this new departure? Because they wish to use the cheaply purchasable votes of the negro freedmen to neutralize the votes of the white working and burgher classes of the North and West, and hope so to use 4,000,000 of negro freedmen as to secure to themselves the power to govern and tax 40,000,000 of whites.

What Attorney-General Akerman says is true: *"Emancipation has* DIVORCED *the interests of* CAPITAL *from the interests of* LABOR." By this divorce the working and burgher classes have lost their *"natural ally."* Now, they must, single-handed and alone, resist the encroachments of power, and the "subtle and artful fiscal contrivances by which capital seeks to divide the wealth of all civilized communities so unequally, and to allot so small a share to those by whose labor it was produced, and so large a share to the non-producing classes."

This divorce was intended to be, and is, complete and perpetual. It is a divorce *a mensa et thoro* and *a vinculo.* There is no appeal. The decree is irreversible, and *it forbids the parties from marrying again.* No one at the North or West, not one in ten thousand at the South, indulges in the delusive dream of a restoration of negro slavery.

What remains? Much of hope and encouragement in the future of the working and burgher classes. With their eyes opened to the *tricks* by which centralism and capital *cajoled* them into a crusade against their natural allies, and by brute force "divorced capital from labor by emancipation," they may find in the experience of the past a light to guide them in the future. If they would successfully resist the encroachments of power, and the artful contrivances of capital, they must go back to the political principles of Washington,

Jefferson, and Calhoun ; principles which Washington, Jefferson, and Calhoun termed *republican*, while the monarchists and capitalists of New England, in derision and by way of reproach, called them *democratic*.

A few more words to the National Labor party. On the 25th of January, 1871, their committee, under a resolution of the National Labor Congress held at Cincinnati, in August, 1870, called a convention to meet *at Columbus, Ohio, at* 10 *o'clock, A. M., on the third Wednesday of October,* 1871, for the purpose of nominating candidates for the offices of President and Vice-President of the United States, and the transaction of such other business as may properly come before them.

On the 29th of May, 1871, H. M. Turner, (negro,) as President of the Georgia State Convention, issued a proclamation addressed " to the *colored citizens* of the States of Alabama, Arkansas, Delaware, Florida, Georgia, Kentucky, Louisiana, Tennessee, Maryland, Mississippi, Missouri, North Carolina, South Carolina, Texas, Virginia, West Virginia, and the Territory of Columbia."

This proclamation calls a convention of the *colored citizens* of the States above named to meet at *Columbia, S. C., on the* 18*th day of October,* 1871, *at* 12 *o'clock, M.*

Now let the working and burgher classes of the North and West take special notice of these dates ! Why this call, in May, 1871, for a negro convention at Columbia on the *same day in October* selected by the committee of the National Labor party as early as January, 1871 ?

It is another *trick* of imperialism and capital to organize the negro vote of all the Southern States in the interest of imperialism and capital, and to neutralize *by that negro vote of the Southern States* any action that may be taken at Columbus, Ohio, by the working and burgher classes of the North and West, against the interests of imperialism and capital.

Look into and think about the purposes and objects of this *little trick !*

BEN. E. GREEN.

WASHINGTON, *June* 12*th,* 1871.

ADDENDA TO TRANSLATOR'S PREFACE.

SUPPLEMENT TO THE FOURTH ANNUAL REPORT OF THE SPECIAL COMMISSIONERS OF THE REVENUE. COST OF LABOR AND SUBSISTENCE IN THE UNITED STATES. TABLES SHOWING THE COMPARATIVE AND AVERAGE WEEKLY WAGES PAID, ETC., ETC. PREPARED BY EDWARD YOUNG, IN CHARGE OF THE BUREAU OF STATISTICS. WASHINGTON: GOVERNMENT PRINTING-OFFICE. 1870.

THE foregoing is the title of an official document sent to us by a Member of Congress,* to convince us, by the statistics it professes to give, that we are wrong in our historic theory that one of the main purposes and results of the late civil war was to reduce wages and increase the cost of living.

On careful examination, we find this document remarkable alike for the absurdity of its multitudinous errors, and for the very manifest purpose of deception, with which it has been carefully and elaborately prepared, as a campaign document, to mislead and *again* betray the working and burgher classes into the support of the (so-*mis*called) Republican party.

In seventy-five octavo pages the Bureau of Statistics gives sixty-seven tables of figures, doubtless supposing that no one would ever take the trouble to wade through them.

The first fifty-eight tables are intended to produce the impression that, under the policy of the (so-*mis*called) Republican Administration, there has been an increase in wages, amounting to an average of forty-eight per cent., as summed up in Table 57, on page 57, as follows :

* Hon. John Coburn, of Indiana.

343

TABLE SHOWING THE PERCENTAGE OF INCREASE IN MONTHLY WAGES, WITH BOARD, PAID FOR FARM AND OTHER LABOR, IN THE UNITED STATES, IN 1869 OVER 1860.

STATES.	Experienced hands (summer.)	Experienced hands (winter.)	Ordinary hands (summer.)	Ordinary hands (winter.)	Common laborers other than farm.	Female servants.	Average increase per cent.
Maine	55	48	45	45	36	44	46
New Hampshire	46	46	45	33	55	64	48
Vermont	65	59	62	59	53	75	62
Massachusetts	60	58	62	76	58	59	62
Rhode Island	57	80	50	100	67	100	75
Connecticut	88	50	67	50	87	75	69
New York	66	57	55	50	55	93	62
New Jersey	81	76	81	81	96	89	84
Pennsylvania	64	70	59	64	51	65	62
Delaware	43	20	50	29	...	100	40
Maryland	67	75	60	50	60	100	69
West Virginia	38	38	40	42	25	40	37
Ohio	48	48	46	45	44	59	48
Indiana	36	60	41	33	42	47	43
Illinois	46	42	42	40	50	69	48
Michigan	62	64	53	60	62	53	59
Wisconsin	42	42	42	31	36	44	39
Minnesota	60	59	66	58	69	59	62
Iowa	50	48	56	51	54	61	53
Kansas	35	69	58	32	48	48	48
Nebraska	83	83	67	50	50	46	63
Missouri	65	37	65	75	63	102	68
Kentucky	28	37	32	20	27	29	29
Virginia	22	15	21	18	15	25	19
North Carolina	40	26	25	15	25	38	28
South Carolina	36	25	33	38	19	50	33
Georgia *	11	20	1	9	10	17	11*
Alabama	30	26	25	27	15	16	23
Mississippi	46	54	46	66	50	20	47
Louisiana	88	85	60	31	34	33	66
Texas	54	71	24	40	38	15	40
Arkansas	35	48	37	66	50	20	43
Tennessee	23	26	27	24	38	40	29
Average in United States, exclusive of Pacific States and the Territories	51	51	47	46	46	51	48

* The percentages of increase here given, although accurately computed, do not indicate the true advance in the wages paid. This arises from the fact that while there were nineteen returns from Georgia giving the wages in 1869, but six of them gave those of 1860. The true increase in the monthly wages paid in 1869 over 1860 was about 23 per cent. instead of 11.

Under the heading, "EXPENSES OF LIVING," Tables 59 to 66, both included, (pages 58 to 73,) are intended to produce the impression that the cost of living has been reduced, while wages have gone up 48 per cent. on an average. In order to make this appear, the Bureau of Statistics selects the years 1867 and 1869 for comparison, and gives prominence to wheat flour, which, for New England, it puts at $12.35 in 1867, and $9.15 in 1869; for the Middle States, at $12.50 in 1867, and $7.85 in 1869; for a portion of the Western

States, at $12.71 in 1867, and $6.41 in 1869; for other Western States and Territories, at $8.67 in 1867, and $5.35 in 1869; and for the Southern States, at $10.72 in 1867, and $9.50 in 1869.

The poet says:

> "Oh! what a tangled web we weave
> When first we practise to deceive."

The Bureau of Statistics, absorbed in its figures, had never read these lines, or did not appreciate the exhortation to honest dealing which they contain; or else it relied on its formidable array of figures to deter any one from attempting to unravel its tangled web of deceit. It is obvious that the Bureau was *"practising to deceive"* when it selected the years 1867 and 1869, and gave this prominence to the varying price of wheat flour, in order to produce the impression on the working and burgher classes that the effect of Radical policy had been to reduce the cost of living. For, this difference in the price of flour was caused, not by any beneficial influence of Radical policy, but partly by the difference in the seasons, and partly by that subtle and artful fiscal contrivance, by which the wheat-growers of the West are placed in the power of the great moneyed aristocracy for the means, with which to move their crops to market; thereby enabling Eastern capital to depress the price of Western wheat at pleasure.

But even admitting that the Bureau's figures are correct and reliable, (which they are not,) they disprove the very idea, which this elaborate document was concocted to sustain. For on pages 74 and 75 we have a table of the "comparative cost of building-materials, and of dwelling-houses," in 1861 and 1869, which shows that "the *true average increase in the cost of materials and labor required in building a dwelling-house suitable for workmen was 88 per cent.*"

Now, this is a much more reliable criterion of the increase or decrease of the cost of living than the difference between the cost of wheat flour in 1867 and 1869; and even if it were true that wages had advanced 48 per cent. from 1860 to 1869, how are the working and burgher classes benefited, when that increase of wages is accompanied by an increase of 88 per cent. in the cost of living?

As to Table 57, page 57, (above quoted,) which pretends to show

23

the percentage of increase in monthly wages, with board, etc., we *know* that in Georgia, where we have lived since 1855, and we *believe* that in the other Southern States, instead of an increase of 23, or even 11 per cent., there has been an actual decrease of from 25 to 50 per cent. on a general average, and not taking into account the exceptional cases of high wages paid for hands in some of the swindling railroad operations, based on State bonds, which, if not repudiated, will bankrupt the States for the profit of a few individual carpet-baggers and scalawags.

Neither can we believe that this table is reliable as to the Eastern, Middle, and Western States.

First, because we *know* that it is wrong as to Georgia, and *believe* it to be wrong as to other Southern States.

Secondly, because it is obviously got up with great care in the interest of the Radical party, and with a premeditated design to "practise to deceive."

Thirdly, because, as the Bureau of Statistics admits, in an introductory note, it is *"the result, mainly, of inquiries made through the assistant assessors of internal revenue in the various collection districts of the United States"*—a very unreliable authority.

Finally, because a mere reading of Table 65, on page 72, which professes to give a summary of the results of all these inquiries and figures, will show to any man of common sense that it is utterly unreliable, not to use the much stronger language which the absurdities of that table would suggest.

It is as follows:

TABLE SHOWING THE AVERAGE WEEKLY EXPENDITURES OF WORKMEN'S FAMILIES IN SOME OF THE MANUFACTURING TOWNS OF THE UNITED STATES IN 1869.

ARTICLES.	Two adults.	Parents and one child.	Parents and two children.	Parents and three children.	Parents and four children.	Parents and five children.	Parents and six children.	Parents and seven children.	Parents and eight children.	General average.	General average in 1867.
Bread and flour........................	$0.75	$0.78	$0.85	$0.95	$1.29	$1.37	$1.73	$2.50	$2.37	$1.39	$1.91
Meat of all kinds....................	1.25	1.60	1.75	1.92	2.21	3.09	2.92	3.07	4.61	2.46	2.46
Lard..	24	33	33	44	40	35	61	33	61	39	33
Butter....................................	1.00	71	82	1.10	1.26	98	1.35	1.34	2.88	1.27	1.12
Cheese....................................	20	12	14	16	20	11	26	24	18	16	26
Sugar and molasses................	69	74	92	92	1.18	85	1.18	76	1.84	1.05	1.01
Milk..	59	41	44	37	50	58	26	56	1.26	55	46
Coffee....................................	30	20	23	32	32	34	34	....	65	3	25
Tea	63	23	39	38	46	57	75	50	35	47	46
Fish, fresh and salt................	10	13	25	20	22	24	23	20	16	19	†
Soap and starch....................	25	17	22	17	23	25	18	16	54	24	29
Salt, pepper, and vinegar......	12	09	08	12	12	11	18	10	20	12	16
Eggs..	30	25	21	24	29	15	06	20	53	25	31
Potatoes and other vegetables	30	44	61	47	73	80	60	40	85	58	61
Fruits, fresh and dried..........	30	26	33	21	42	46	27	50	62	39	56
Fuel..	1.00	96	74	1.09	1.20	1.13	85	1.21	1.50	1.05	91
Oil or other light	30	22	25	23	21	23	19	16	22	22	22
Other articles........................	1.11	22	54	21	21	20	35	....	38	35	73
Spirits, beer, and tobacco......	....	23	02	13	35	47	27	05	12	16	†
House rent..............................	*4.50	2.17	2.23	2.29	2.17	*3.34	2.25	2.25	2.56	2.64	2 14
Taxes......................................	....	37	03	12	05	24	18	....	30	13	†
For benevolent objects..........	39	34	58	40	34	25	30	2.00	60	57	†
Total per week (clothing excepted)............................	14.32	10.97	11.96	12.44	13.36	16.11	15.36	16.42	25.44	14.93	14.29

* The increased cost of house rent, and the use of more expensive provisions, render the expenses of these families higher than some of larger size.

† Not furnished in 1867. Deducting these, the average weekly expenses of families in 1869, as compared with 1867, will be reduced to $13.88.

This table presents results that would make Malthus, dead as he is, open his eyes with astonishment. We earnestly recommend to all, who are contemplating obedience to the Scriptural injunction, "*increase and multiply*," to study it carefully. It would be too tedious to point out all its peculiarities. A few will suffice to direct attention to the others.

1st. According to this table, the average expense per week of a workman and wife with seven children for bread and flour is $2.50; with eight children, only $2.37.

2d. With six children, their average weekly expense for lard will be 63 cents; with seven children, only 33 cents.

3d. Their average weekly expense for butter will be, without children, $1.00; with one child, only 71 cents; with two children, 82 cents; with three children, $1.10; with four children, $1.26; with five children, only 98 cents, etc., etc.

4th. Their average weekly expense for cheese will be, without children, 20 cents; with one child, 12 cents; with two children, 14 cents; with three children, 16 cents; with four children, 20 cents; with five children, 11 cents; and with eight children, 18 cents.

5th. Their average weekly expense, without children, for sugar and molasses, will be 69 cents; with four children, $1.18; with seven children, only 76 cents.

6th. Their average weekly expense for milk will be, without children, 59 cents; with one child, 41 cents; with two children, 44 cents; with three children, 37 cents; with four children, 50 cents; with five children, 58 cents; with six children, 26 cents; with seven children, 56 cents; and with eight children, $1.26.

Finally, and funniest of all — even funnier than the allowance, on a general average, of 59 cents for milk to a workman and wife without children, and only 26 cents for a workman and wife with six children — is the Bureau's estimate for soap and starch:

It allows to a man and wife without children, per week	25 cents.
"	"	"	with 1 child,	"	17	"
"	"	"	"	2 children,	"	22	"
"	"	"	"	3	"	"	17	"
"	"	"	"	4	"	"	23	"
"	"	"	"	5	"	"	25	"
"	"	"	"	6	"	"	18	"
"	"	"	"	7	"	"	16	"
"	"	"	"	8	"	"	54	"

Without wasting more time, the reader will find similar absurdities running through the whole of this and other tables of this precious production of the Radical Bureau of Statistics. It might excite merriment and laughter, if indignation at such palpable partisan patchwork would admit of pleasantry. But the question is too serious for mirth. These tables have been laboriously prepared in the interest of the monarchical, aristocratic, *cheap-labor* party, and on the supposition that the great mass of the people of the United States — lawyers, doctors, ministers of the gospel, merchants, civil engineers, etc., etc., as well as the working-men — were too busy with their own private affairs, or too ignorant, to discover and expose the deceit attempted to be practised upon them by this array of figures.

When we examined the figures, we thought, *surely*, these must be typographical errors. We therefore called upon Mr. Edward Young, at the Bureau of Statistics, in the Treasury Department, and asked him whether there were any typographical errors in his tables. He said, "No." We then asked him to explain by what process of computation he arrived at such wonderful results, according to which a husband and wife, without children, required 25 cents' worth of soap and starch per week ; with one child, only 17 cents; with six children, 18 cents ; and with seven childen, only 16 cents.

The reply, not very courteously given, was : "That table has been criticized before, and where there is a determination to criticize, anything may be criticized." Pursuing information under difficulties, we persisted, and at last drew out this explanation, viz. that the first nine columns of figures do not represent *averages*, as the heading would indicate, but only the expenditures of single selected families, the *averages* being given in the tenth and eleventh columns, so as to show a reduction in the cost of living from 1867 to 1869.

Our interview with the Bureau of Statistics convinced us that its tables were manufactured solely for partisan purposes, and are utterly unreliable, except in so far as they show, on page 75, that the true average increase in the cost of materials and labor required in building a dwelling-house suitable for workmen has been 88 per cent. in the ten years that the so-miscalled Republican party have been in power.

CONTENTS.

CHAPTER I.

GENERAL IDEA OF THE PROLETARIAT.

The working classes do not exist among all peoples — Why? — No one has
dreamed of writing their history — Gap which the absence of that history
leaves in politics — The working classes come from the proletariat — Modern signification of this word — The proletariat comprises working-men,

CHAPTER II.

ORIGIN OF THE PROLETARIAT.

Political prejudices which the history of the four branches of the proletariat
ought to dispel — The proletariat produced by the emancipation of slaves
— Among all peoples before the emancipation of slaves there were neither
working-men, nor beggars, nor thieves, nor prostitutes — Why? — By Chris-
tianity the proletaries greatly multiplied — Slavery having preceded the
proletariat among all peoples, whence comes that universal slavery which

CHAPTER III.

ORIGIN OF SLAVERY.

The first epoch of every society contains two classes of men, masters and
slaves — This fact anterior to all institutions, and therefore not instituted
— In what sense slavery may be said to be by divine right — Slavery is a
primitive and spontaneous element of all societies — The history of the
masters gives the history of the slaves — Whence come masters? — The
first masters the first fathers — Of the paternal power in noble families —
Names designating these families in the Greek and Latin poets — Signification of the word *pius* — Paternal power absolute in noble families —

CHAPTER IV.

ORGANIZATION OF SLAVERY BY POSITIVE LAWS.

CHAPTER V.

EMANCIPATION OF SLAVES AND FORMATION OF BURGHERS.

CHAPTER VI.

GENERAL IDEA OF THE COMMUNE — TWO KINDS.

CHAPTER VII.

THE FRENCH COMMUNE.

CHAPTER VIII.

SYMPTOMS OF THE ANCIENT COMMUNE — HIRELINGS AND BEGGARS.

CHAPTER IX.

SYMPTOMS OF THE ANCIENT COMMUNE — ARCHITECTURE.

CHAPTER X.

SYMPTOMS OF THE ANCIENT COMMUNE — JURISPRUDENCE.

CHAPTER XI.

THE PEASANTS.

CHAPTER XII.

ANCIENT TRADES' UNIONS — FORMATION.

CHAPTER XIII.

ANCIENT TRADES' UNIONS — DEVELOPMENT.

CHAPTER XIV.

ANCIENT TRADES' UNIONS — THEIR FALL.

CHAPTER XV.

BEGGARS AND HOSPITALS.

CHAPTER XVI.

LITERARY SLAVES.

CHAPTER XVII.

THE COURTESANS.

CHAPTER XVIII.

BANDITS.

CHAPTER XIX.

MODERN TRADES' UNIONS.

CHAPTER XX.

INDEX

TO

TRANSLATOR'S PREFACE AND NOTES.

FINIS.

THE

IRREPRESSIBLE CONFLICT

BETWEEN

LABOR AND CAPITAL:

A BRIEF SUMMARY OF SOME OF THE CHIEF CAUSES AND
RESULTS OF THE LATE CIVIL WAR IN THE
UNITED STATES,

AS PRESENTED IN

THE TRANSLATOR'S PREFACE

TO

ADOLPHE GRANIER DE CASSAGNAC'S

HISTORY OF THE WORKING AND BURGHER CLASSES,

IN WHICH THE

ORIGIN, NATURE, AND OBJECTS OF THE MUCH CALUMNIATED
FRENCH COMMUNE
ARE HISTORICALLY EXPLAINED.

PHILADELPHIA:
CLAXTON, REMSEN & HAFFELFINGER,
819 & 821 MARKET STREET.
1872.

HISTORY OF THE
WORKING AND BURGHER CLASSES.

BY M. ADOLPHE GRANIER DE CASSAGNAC,
PARIS, FRANCE, A. D. 1838.

TRANSLATED BY BEN. E. GREEN,
OF DALTON, WHITFIELD CO., GA.

Published by CLAXTON, REMSEN & HAFFELFINGER, Philadelphia.

From the Washington Chronicle.

This valuable work has been for some time out of print, and copies of it are exceedingly rare, therefore an American translation will be welcome.

From the New Orleans Times.

Cassagnac wrote this elaborate history in two parts, the first of which is now translated ; the second, on the " Noble Classes," is, we believe, extant only in the original French. It has not been our fortune before this to meet with the work, although at the period of its publication in Paris it commanded attention, and has been ever since the source of nearly all the discussions on the great social and political questions of the conflict between monarchy and democracy, and capital and labor — two elements of strife that, alike in Europe and this country, are rapidly assuming portentous shapes, and which cannot be put aside even by the most indolent observer. When we opened this volume, we at once remembered the notices that appeared in one of the French periodicals, and now are satisfied that, *of its class, it is the most profound and exhaustive.* We urge any of our citizens who think about the results of business, or the near future of the United States, both politically and financially, to buy this volume and ponder its contents.

From the Trenton Gazette.

This work of Adolphe Cassagnac is an interesting and instructive work. It abounds with classical lore and curious information, and to the student of the labor problem is a treasure.

From the Atlanta Constitution, Atlanta, Ga.

This work is an intensely interesting one. The preface of the translator, Mr. Ben. E. Green, of this State, is a very elaborate one, setting forth, among other propositions, the causes of the late war, the effect of negro slavery in the South, the struggle of classes in this as in all other countries, the fusion of elements producing the Republican party, and that emancipation has cheapened labor, reducing its wages and diminishing its share of the products. The Translator thinks that even Mr. Stephens has not reached the real causes of the war, which are claimed to be the " Conflict between Monarchy and Democracy," and the " Irrepressible desire of capital to cheapen labor." In " The Laboring and Burgher Classes " are included all the learned professions — all who labor with the brain or with the hand, and who wish to live and grow rich by the fruits of their own honest industry. De Cassagnac was a student " absorbed in the solution of the facts and philosophy of history." He has treated his subject exhaustingly, and with great faithfulness as a historian. The work is an exceedingly valuable one, and should find its way into every library. The Preface alone is worth the price of the book.

www.ingramcontent.com/pod-product-compliance
Lightning Source LLC
Chambersburg PA
CBHW032356280326
41935CB00008B/596